how2become.com

TRAIN DRIVER SITUATIONAL JUDGEMENT TESTS

www.How2Become.com

Orders: Please contact How2become Ltd, Suite 1, 60 Churchill Square Business Centre, Kings Hill, Kent ME19 4YU.

Please order via the email address: info@how2become.com.

ISBN: 978-1-910602-88-1

First published 2016

Copyright © 2016 How2Become Ltd.

All rights reserved. Apart from any permitted use under UK copyright law, no part of this publication may be reproduced or transmitted in any form or by any means, electronic or mechanical, including photocopying, recording, or any information, storage or retrieval system, without permission in writing from the publisher or under licence from the Copyright Licensing Agency Limited. Further details of such licenses (for reprographic reproduction) may be obtained from the Copyright Licensing Agency Ltd, Saffron House, 6-10 Kirby Street, London EC1N 8TS.

Typeset for How2become Ltd Anton Pshinka.

Printed and bound by CPI Group (UK) Ltd, Croydon, CR0 4YY

CONTENTS

INTRODUCTION 5

SITUATIONAL JUDGEMENT TESTS 7

TEST 1 (Train Driver related) 15

      SUGGESTED ANSWERS TEST 1 63

TEST 2 (Non Train Driver related) 72

      SUGGESTED ANSWERS TEST 2 117

TEST 3 (Non Train Driver related) 163

      SUGGESTED ANSWERS TEST 3 187

Serious about applying for Train Driver selection?

Attend a 1-day Train Driver training course with our expert tutors.

Visit the following website to find out more:

www.TrainDriverCourse.co.uk

INTRODUCTION

Welcome to your new guide, *Train Driver Situational Judgement Tests*. This guide has been designed to help you prepare for the situational judgement test element of the new Trainee Train Driver assessment. The guide contains lots of sample questions, answers and advice to help you gain the required pass mark for becoming a Trainee Train Driver with any of the UK-based Train Operating Companies (TOCs).

The author of this guide, Richard McMunn, has over twenty years' experience in recruitment. In particular, he has vast experience and knowledge in the area of Train Driver recruitment, and you will find his guidance both inspiring and highly informative.

Whilst the selection process for becoming a Trainee Train Driver is highly competitive, there are a number of things that you can do to increase your chances of success, and they are all contained within the guides and services we provide at How2Become.com.

The guide itself has been split up into useful sections to make it easier for you to prepare for the test. Read each section carefully and take notes as you progress. Don't ever give up on your dream; if you really want to become a Train Driver, then you CAN do it. The way to approach an application for a job of this nature is to embark on a programme of 'in-depth' preparation, and this guide will show you exactly how to do that.

If you need any further help with the Train Driver tests, application form or interview, then here at How2Become we offer a wide range of products and courses to assist you. These are all available through our online shop at **www.How2Become.com**.

We are also now running a number of 1-day intensive Trainee Train Driver training courses at the following website:

www.TrainDriverCourse.co.uk

Once again, thank you for your custom and we wish you all the best in your pursuit of becoming a Train Driver.

Work hard, stay focused and be what you want!

Best wishes,

The How2become Team

SITUATIONAL JUDGEMENT TESTS

SITUATIONAL JUDGEMENT TESTS

Train Operating Companies in the UK are starting to use a form of situational judgement test as part of the assessment criteria for assessing Trainee Train Drivers. Another name for this type of new test is the '*TDSJT*'.

The TDSJT was introduced as an additional way to help TOCs assess the safe working capabilities of potential Train Drivers. During the old assessment format, most people who attended the Train Driver interview would pass (over 90%) and so a new series of tests was introduced to improve the quality of assessment.

The purpose of this book is to provide you with some invaluable sample questions that will help you prepare for the real test. Within this book we have provided you with different types of situational judgement test questions; ones which are Train Driver related, and ones which are not Train Driver related, and are therefore 'generic' in nature.

The reason for the different types of questions is simple; we want you to experience alternative types and formats of situational judgement questioning prior to the real assessment. This will enable you to be better prepared for the test itself.

On that basis, make sure you attempt and understand each type of question format before you attend the Trainee Train Driver assessment day. In addition to practising the questions within this book, be sure to try out the practice questions sent to you by the Train Operating Company to which you have applied.

THE IMPORTANCE OF SITUATIONAL JUDGEMENT TESTS

The reason that this test has been introduced is so that Train Operating Companies (TOCs) can determine how candidates are **likely** to perform in a safety-critical role. As you will be fully aware, the Rail Industry has an excellent safety record and the assessment of candidates in relation to their 'safe working capabilities', is paramount.

SITUATIONAL JUDGEMENT TESTS

This form of situational judgement test has been used for many years in other safety-critical roles, such as the Police Service and the Fire Service.

The questions are usually presented in the same format. You are required to read a passage and then decide which of the presented four options you would most likely carry out first, second, third and fourth. First being the option you feel is MOST appropriate, and fourth being the option you feel is LEAST appropriate. Within this guide we have provided you with a variety of questions and testing formats to ensure you are fully prepared. On that basis, make sure you read the instructions carefully prior to each test section.

The TDSJT is a very strong indicator of how a Trainee Train Driver would likely perform in any given situation. Of course, the situational judgement test for Train Drivers is not a perfect assessment, simply because it is very difficult to replicate the highly pressurised environment in which a Train Driver would find themselves. However, applicants are required to take this assessment under timed conditions, which adds its own element of pressure for you to overcome.

SAMPLE TRAIN DRIVER SITUATIONAL JUDGEMENT TEST

The following is a sample TDSJT question for you to try. Following the question is a breakdown of how the answer has been reached.

> **NOTE:** The following sample questions are the copyright of How2Become Ltd and are not to be reproduced without permission.

Sample question

> You are driving a train and you are approaching the platform at Preston train station when you realise there is a person up ahead on the track. What would you do?

A. Immediately apply the emergency brake before informing the Rail Safety Centre (RSC) of the situation.

B. Inform the Rail Safety Centre and wait for instructions on what to do next.

C. Allow the train to come to a safe stop using the normal braking procedure. Any sudden braking is likely to cause disruption and potential injury to the passengers.

D. Allow the train to come to a safe stop using the normal braking procedure before informing the Rail Safety Centre.

SITUATIONAL JUDGEMENT TESTS

ANSWER OPTIONS IN ORDER OR PRIORITY

A – First

D – Second

C – Third

B – Fourth

How to tackle the question

Whenever you are answering this type of Train Driver related situational judgement question, always focus on SAFETY. Ask yourself the following questions when looking at the four presented options:

Q. *Which of the four presented options is the safest?*

Q. *Which of the four presented options looks most likely to be taught during initial Trainee Train Driver training?*

Q. *Which of the four presented options appears to be the most dangerous?*

In the above question, **Option A** states that you would:

'Immediately apply the emergency brake before informing the Rail Safety Centre (RSC) of the situation.'

- This response clearly applies the **most effective** use of safe-operating procedures and is most likely to be taught during training.

Conversely, **Option B**, whilst having an element of safety to it (you are informing the Rail Safety Centre), does not do anything to stop the train, resulting in possible injuries or death to the person on the track.

Answer **Option D**, **Option C** and **Option B** will very likely result in the death or very serious injury to the person on the track; therefore, these options should be your second, third and fourth choices, respectively.

TIPS FOR PASSING THE SITUATIONAL JUDGEMENT TEST

There are a number of things you can do in order to help improve your scores during the TDSJT. The following tips will help you to prepare effectively and improve your overall ability to pass this type of psychometric test:

TIP 1 – There are many types of situational judgement tests available on the market. Just because you are applying to become a Train Driver, doesn't mean you should focus solely on Train Driver related SJTs. Obtain as many SJT questions as possible from a variety of different genres, and practice accordingly.

TIP 2 – When you read the question you will be presented with a 'situation'. Read the situation quickly before scanning each of the presented options. Look for the safest option first (OPTION 1) and then look for the option you would be least likely to carry out (OPTION 4). Then, assess the final two options (OPTIONS 2 & 3) and place them in order of priority based on what you would do in that type of situation.

TIP 3 – You do not need to be a Train Driver in order to pass the Train Driver related situational judgement test questions provided within this book. What you do need to be is safety-conscious and have a good level of common sense. When assessing the situation and presented options, always err on the side of safety. **Remember** – safety is absolutely paramount at all times in the Railway Industry; whether it's the safety of your passengers, yourself, your work colleagues or the rolling stock you are responsible for. Under no circumstances should you put your passengers, crew or rolling stock in danger.

TIP 4 – Be entirely honest in how you answer the questions. This is very important. The role of a Train Driver involves a high degree of trust, integrity, professionalism, safety and a strict adherence to rules and procedures. The test is designed to assess how you would perform or react to given situations. You should also be aware that the Train Operating Company may ask you questions during the interview based on the answers you provide during the situational judgement test. For example, if you answer a question during the

SITUATIONAL JUDGEMENT TESTS

TDSJT that indicates you prefer to work alone as opposed to working as part of a team, yet you contradict yourself during one of the interview questions and state you prefer to work as part of a team, this could lose you marks and imply you are dishonest. By answering the questions honestly during the test, you will not have to worry about how you answer the questions during the interview.

TIP 5 – Preparation is key! In the weeks leading up to your test, work hard to improve your skills in the testing areas. In addition to the tests contained within this guide, there are numerous other testing resources available at www.How2Become.com. Try out as many test questions as possible and make sure you learn from your mistakes.

TIP 6 – Get a good night's sleep before the test day and don't drink any alcohol or caffeine in the build up to the tests. It is important that you drink plenty of water in order to keep yourself hydrated.

TIP 7 – On the morning of the test, get up early and have a final run through of some sample test questions, just to get your brain working.

TIP 8 – Eat a good healthy breakfast such as bran flakes and a chopped-up banana. Don't eat anything too heavy that will make you feel bloated or sluggish. Remember, you want to be at your best.

TIP 9 – Wear a smart, formal outfit for the testing day. The reason for this is some candidates will be casually dressed. However, you are applying for a professional career and therefore appearance is important. It is better to stand out for the right reasons. As a Train Driver you are a role model for the Train Operating Company you are applying to join. Make the effort to dress smart.

TIP 10 – On the day of your test, check the news for any potential traffic problems and leave in good time to arrive at the test centre with plenty of time to spare. Take a small bottle of water with you to help keep you hydrated.

Now move onto the first testing section of the guide. There are 40 sample test questions and you have 40 minutes to complete them. Suggested answers are provided immediately after the test.

TEST 1

(Train Driver related)

TEST 1 (TRAIN DRIVER RELATED)

There are 40 questions in the following test and you have 40 minutes to complete them all.

When answering the questions in this particular test, state which option you would choose first, second, third and finally fourth.

A box is provided below each question for you to insert your chosen answers.

> **DISCLAIMER:** The incidents and scenarios provided within the following test are entirely fictitious in nature. They are not intended to be representative of the role of a Train Driver, or the rules and procedures one would follow when employed by a Train Operating Company.

TEST 1 (Train Driver related)

QUESTION 1

> Whilst serving as a fully qualified Train Driver, you become concerned that the standard of continuous professional development training has been dropping over the last few months. What do you do?

ANSWER OPTIONS

A. Provide feedback to your manager on how you believe the training could be improved in order to improve safety.

B. At the end of the day, any issues surrounding training standards are down to the line manager. It is up to them to sort it out, and if they can't recognise there's an issue, then that's not your problem.

C. Apply for promotion so that you can be in charge of training and therefore improve the standards.

D. Discuss your concerns with the other Train Drivers first. If they agree with you, then inform your manager.

ANSWER OPTIONS IN ORDER OF PRIORITY

1st	
2nd	
3rd	
4th	

TRAIN DRIVER SITUATIONAL JUDGEMENT TESTS

QUESTION 2

> Whilst preparing the train at Euston Station for your regular weekly journey to Glasgow Central, the train guard approaches you in the cab to inform you that there are problems with the train's communication system. He tells you that no announcements will be able to be made to passengers during the journey because of the fault. What would you do?

ANSWER OPTIONS

A. Thank the guard for the information and carry on with your duties preparing the train.

B. Thank the guard for the information before informing the station manager about the defect. You will not be able to drive this train, as you will not be able to make any safety-related announcements to the passengers during the journey, if the need arises. The safety of the passengers and the other crew members is paramount.

C. Thank the guard for the information before heading off to see if you can fix the problem yourself. You are a Train Driver, and as such, you are a highly practical and adaptable person. You are confident you can fix the problem before the train departs the platform. If you can't fix it, you will then inform your station manager of the problem.

D. Thank the guard for the information before informing him that you will contact him directly if any important announcements need to be made during the journey. If there are any announcements that need to be made, the guard can then walk up and down the train carriages informing the passengers. The most important thing is to ensure the passengers receive all important messages.

TEST 1 (Train Driver related)

ANSWER OPTIONS IN ORDER OF PRIORITY

1st	
2nd	
3rd	
4th	

QUESTION 3

> You wake up one morning and start to get ready for work. You are scheduled to drive the 10:05 train from Paddington to Reading. All of a sudden you start to feel ill and uneasy. Whilst driving to work your eyes become slightly blurred, but you are just about OK to drive. When you arrive at work you still feel slightly ill. What would you do?

ANSWER OPTIONS

A. Immediately inform your manager about how you feel and that you think you're OK to drive the train.

B. Battle through it. You are a Train Driver and you have a responsibility to drive the train on time, so that the passengers get to their destination.

C. Take headache tablets and monitor the situation. If you feel bad during the journey from Paddington to Reading, then you will consider booking sick once you reach Reading.

D. Immediately book sick so that a replacement driver can be found, before informing your line manager.

ANSWER OPTIONS IN ORDER OF PRIORITY

1st	
2nd	
3rd	
4th	

TEST 1 (Train Driver related)

QUESTION 4

You are a fully qualified and experienced Train Driver. You are sat around the station canteen mess table having a cup of tea with some other Train Drivers. There's a bit of banter going on and one of the more senior Train Drivers is making fun out of a newly qualified Train Driver. The new Train Driver appears to be slightly upset by the comments but doesn't say anything. What would you do?

ANSWER OPTIONS

A. Intervene and say that you do not think the comments are appropriate. Even though the driver is new, that doesn't mean he should be the centre of any harmful jokes or comments.

B. Banter is all part of railway working life. Train Drivers work in lonely and highly pressurised situations and a bit of canteen banter is good for morale. If the new Train Driver is going to fit in, then he will need to get used to it.

C. Leave the canteen and go and inform your station manager of the comments.

D. You would probably join in with the banter.

ANSWER OPTIONS IN ORDER OF PRIORITY

1st	
2nd	
3rd	
4th	

QUESTION 5

> You are driving a train with Overhead Line Equipment (OLE) between Slough and Paddington when you suddenly notice in the distance a metal scaffolding bar hanging from the catenary wire. The metal scaffolding bar looks like it will hit your cab screen window. What would you do?

ANSWER OPTIONS

A. Immediately bring the train to a safe stop and report the incident to the signaller and the Electrical Control Operator (ECO). You would then follow your training and inform the guard and passengers that you had to stop due to an incident and that you would update them as soon as you had any further information. Under no circumstances would you leave the cab, for safety reasons.

B. Immediately bring the train to a safe stop and report the incident to the signaller and the Electrical Control Operator (ECO). You would then follow your training and inform the guard and passengers that you had to stop due to an incident and that you would update them as soon as you had any further information. You would then leave the cab to assess the situation and see if it was possible to remove the metal bar yourself.

C. Immediately bring the train to a safe stop. You would then leave the cab to assess the situation and see if it was possible to remove the metal bar yourself. This way, you would be able to get moving again quickly to ensure all passengers arrived at their destination on time.

D. As you understand, responsibility for safety rests with the train guard, and as such, he/she would be responsible for dealing with this type of incident. You would stop the train and then would ask them what they intended to do about it.

TEST 1 (Train Driver related) 23

ANSWER OPTIONS IN ORDER OF PRIORITY

1st	
2nd	
3rd	
4th	

TRAIN DRIVER SITUATIONAL JUDGEMENT TESTS

QUESTION 6

> You are driving a train from Preston train station to Blackpool Central. A few minutes into your journey you notice that the Driver Safety Device (DSD) stops working. What would you do?

ANSWER OPTIONS

A. Do nothing. The train can still operate and you feel fine. The journey from Preston to Blackpool is short, so it won't be long before you arrive there anyway.

B. Immediately make a note of this in your log book and inform your station manager when you return to Preston later.

C. Immediately inform the signaller so they can advise you what to do next. They will either advise how the train can continue safely or inform you where/when to stop so a proper assessment can be made.

D. Stop the train immediately and then inform the signaller.

ANSWER OPTIONS IN ORDER OF PRIORITY

1st	
2nd	
3rd	
4th	

QUESTION 7

> You are currently sat at the train station waiting to depart when you notice your cab windscreen is dirty. You try to wash the windows using the in-built wash system but it appears not to be working. What would you do?

ANSWER OPTIONS

A. Go outside the cab, and attempt to clean it yourself with a dry rag.

B. Inform the train guard so that he can get assistance for you and get someone to clean the windscreen and repair the in-built wash system.

C. Follow your training and the rule book and inform the relevant person(s) so that the window can be cleaned and the in-built wash system repaired before you set off.

D. Do nothing. This type of thing happens all of the time. It's scheduled to rain during the journey so the screen should get cleaned anyway.

ANSWER OPTIONS IN ORDER OF PRIORITY

1st	
2nd	
3rd	
4th	

TRAIN DRIVER SITUATIONAL JUDGEMENT TESTS

QUESTION 8

> You are a qualified Train Driver and you are driving to work one day. All of a sudden, approximately one mile from work, there is a serious accident up ahead and traffic comes to a complete standstill. After 10 minutes of waiting, the traffic has not moved and there is a danger you will be late for work. What would you do?

ANSWER OPTIONS

A. Carry on waiting in your car.

B. Use your mobile phone to call one of your colleagues and ask them if they can cover your shift.

C. Use your mobile phone to call your supervisory manager to inform him/her that there is a possibility you will be late for work due to traffic. This will allow them sufficient time to find an alternative driver.

D. Pull over to a safe place at the side of the road where you can legally park, get out of your car, lock it and then proceed on foot to the train station. Train Drivers are never late and you do not intend on being late for your shift as this will impact your passengers.

ANSWER OPTIONS IN ORDER OF PRIORITY

1st	
2nd	
3rd	
4th	

TEST 1 (Train Driver related)

QUESTION 9

> You are sat at home one Saturday evening. It is 8pm and you have had one pint of lager when the phone rings. It is your supervisory manager. She informs you that one of the Train Drivers has called in sick and they are desperate to find another driver to cover the shift. She asks if you would cover the shift in return for double pay. What would you do?

ANSWER OPTIONS

A. Immediately agree to cover the shift and make your way to work. Flexibility is one of the key requirements of a Train Driver.

B. Tell her you are unable to cover the shift because you have had a drink of alcohol and it would not be safe for you to drive the train.

C. Tell her you have had one drink of alcohol, but that you feel fine and are happy to cover the shift.

D. Immediately agree to cover the shift and make your way to work by public transport. By the time you arrive at work, you will have sobered up.

ANSWER OPTIONS IN ORDER OF PRIORITY

1st	
2nd	
3rd	
4th	

TRAIN DRIVER SITUATIONAL JUDGEMENT TESTS

QUESTION 10

You are a Train Driver with over 10 years' experience. A new Trainee Train Driver approaches you and she asks for help with route learning. What would you do?

ANSWER OPTIONS

A. Agree to help her with the route learning. You can remember how difficult it was when you were learning the routes. You would be more than happy to assist.

B. Tell her that you are not paid to train new Trainee Train Drivers. You get paid to drive the trains, not teach people how to drive them.

C. Tell her that she will need to ask her line manager as you don't want to give her the wrong information.

D. Tell her that you personally don't believe women should be driving trains and that you are unable to assist her.

ANSWER OPTIONS IN ORDER OF PRIORITY

1st	
2nd	
3rd	
4th	

TEST 1 (Train Driver related)

QUESTION 11

> You have been serving as a Train Driver for 6 years and are a respected member of the Train Operating Company. Your station manager approaches you and asks you to take under your wing a newly qualified Train Driver who has just joined the team that same day. You start talking to him, whilst showing him around the train station, and he confides in you that he is gay. He tells you that he is worried what the other Train Drivers will say, and asks for your advice. What would you do?

ANSWER OPTIONS

A. Tell him that his sexual orientation is not a problem and makes no difference to how he will be treated at work. If he does have any problems, then he can come to you or the station manager immediately for support and advice.

B. Tell him that, because we all work closely together at times, it would be best if he kept his secret to himself. The other Train Drivers might be offended. Providing that he doesn't make any advances on you, and keeps himself to himself, then it shouldn't be a problem.

C. Immediately tell the line manager so that he/she can decide what to say to him. You wouldn't want to give him the wrong advice and risk upsetting him.

D. Tell him that he will probably get a bit of stick from the other Train Drivers, but that means that they will like him and that he'll be popular.

TRAIN DRIVER SITUATIONAL JUDGEMENT TESTS

ANSWER OPTIONS IN ORDER OF PRIORITY

1st	
2nd	
3rd	
4th	

TEST 1 (Train Driver related)

QUESTION 12

You are waiting to pull away from Salisbury train station but the train conductor has not given you the signal to pull away. You look in your cab mirror and notice that the conductor has boarded the train. It appears that all passengers have also now boarded the train. What would you do?

ANSWER OPTIONS

A. The train conductor has most probably forgotten to give you the signal, or you didn't see/hear it. Because the conductor has boarded the train, you would pull away safely.

B. You would sit in your cab and not move until you received the signal from the conductor. It would be dangerous to pull away without confirmation that it is safe to do so and all of the doors have been closed.

C. You would sit in your cab and not move until you received the signal from the conductor. If you believed that the signal to pull away had not been given, you would establish contact with the train conductor to ascertain what the situation was regarding the boarding of the train and the closing of the doors. It would be dangerous to pull away without confirmation that it is safe to do so and all of the doors have been closed and under no circumstances would you put anyone in danger.

D. You would immediately establish contact with the train conductor to ascertain what the situation was regarding the boarding of the train and the closing of the doors. It would be dangerous to pull away without confirmation that it is safe to do so and all of the doors have been closed. Under no circumstances would you put anyone in danger.

TRAIN DRIVER SITUATIONAL JUDGEMENT TESTS

ANSWER OPTIONS IN ORDER OF PRIORITY

1st	
2nd	
3rd	
4th	

TEST 1 (Train Driver related)

QUESTION 13

> Whilst at the train station in the locker room, you overhear a conversation between two Train Drivers. One of them is making inappropriate comments centred around the other Train Driver's gender. What would you do?

ANSWER OPTIONS

A. Ignore the comments and carry on with your work.

B. Join in with the comments. It's only a bit of fun and if the other person cannot take it, then they shouldn't be in the job.

C. Immediately challenge the inappropriate behaviour and explain how the comments are not in line with company policy.

D. Report the comments to your line manager. It is their responsibility to deal with this kind of issue.

ANSWER OPTIONS IN ORDER OF PRIORITY

1st	
2nd	
3rd	
4th	

QUESTION 14

A fellow Train Driver has been absent due to sickness and she has missed an important CPD (Continuous Professional Development) update that has highlighted a number of important changes to company policy. What would you do?

ANSWER OPTIONS

A. Immediately explain to her what the changes are and clarify that she fully understands them.

B. Inform your station manager of her absence so that he can tell her what they are.

C. Do nothing. She will probably find out about the changes through other work colleagues or whilst she is going about her daily work routine.

D. Do nothing. It's not your responsibility to inform her of CPD updates. Someone else gets paid to do that job.

ANSWER OPTIONS IN ORDER OF PRIORITY

1st	
2nd	
3rd	
4th	

TEST 1 (Train Driver related)

QUESTION 15

A fellow Train Driver work colleague, who is from a different ethnic background to yourself, asks you if you would cover one of their shifts whilst they pray. What would you do?

ANSWER OPTIONS

A. This has got nothing to do with work and therefore they should not be allowed time during working hours to pray. You don't personally pray, so why should they be allowed? You would not cover their shift under any circumstances.

B. You would be happy to cover their shift if they promised to pay you for it.

C. You would be happy to cover their shift if they promised to pay back the time at a later date.

D. You would be happy to cover their shift as you understand that, as part of their religious beliefs, they need time to pray.

ANSWER OPTIONS IN ORDER OF PRIORITY

1st	
2nd	
3rd	
4th	

QUESTION 16

> You are carrying out checks in your train cab prior to a journey when you notice one of the safety-critical cab dials is inoperative. What would you do?

ANSWER OPTIONS

A. Immediately inform your station manager so that the dial could either be repaired or a replacement train sought. Under no circumstances would you drive the train with defective dials, unless otherwise instructed to do so.

B. Carry on with your journey. There are many dials in the train cab and you assume the dial will get repaired during its next service.

C. Ask an engineer for his/her view on what to do.

D. Attempt to fix the dial yourself. If you couldn't fix it, you would ask for help.

ANSWER OPTIONS IN ORDER OF PRIORITY

1st	
2nd	
3rd	
4th	

QUESTION 17

You are the driver of a passenger train and you are starting to pull out of the station. As you increase speed, you notice there is a damaged part of the track on the opposite side to the track you are travelling on. There is a member of staff standing at the end of the station platform watching you pull away. What would you do?

ANSWER OPTIONS

A. Try to get the station platform staff's attention and indicate to him that there is a damaged part of the track on the opposite side. Then, make contact with the signaller to inform him/her of the damaged track and its location.

B. Immediately raise the alarm by communicating with the signaller and informing him/her of the damaged track and its location.

C. Do nothing. It is likely that the station platform assistant would have noticed the damaged track and they will be raising the alarm very soon.

D. Immediately stop the train before getting out of your cab and to double check that there is actually a damaged part of the track. The last thing you want to do is raise the alarm and stop any oncoming trains, if there isn't any damage.

ANSWER OPTIONS IN ORDER OF PRIORITY

1st	
2nd	
3rd	
4th	

QUESTION 18

> You are the driver of a passenger train and you are just about to pull out of the station when a member of the public runs up to your cab window and tells you there is a fire on the embankment approximately 50 yards down from the end of the platform. What would you do?

ANSWER OPTIONS

A. Immediately contact the signaller and the Rail Safety Centre and inform them of the fire.

B. Use your mobile phone to call the Fire Service before commencing your journey.

C. Do nothing. It is likely that the station platform assistant will notice the fire and they will take the necessary action.

D. Ask the member of public to use their mobile phone to call the Fire Service before commencing with your journey. Once you have pulled away from the station, you will then contact the signaller and the Rail Safety Centre.

ANSWER OPTIONS IN ORDER OF PRIORITY

1st	
2nd	
3rd	
4th	

TEST 1 (Train Driver related)

QUESTION 19

> You are a Trainee Train Driver part-way through your initial training. You are sat taking an important safety-related examination when you notice a fellow Trainee Train Driver sat next to you, cheating. What would you do?

ANSWER OPTIONS

A. It really isn't any of your business. If he wants to cheat, so be it. He will eventually get caught out and the rail staff will soon realise he cannot do his job properly.

B. Wait to see whether or not he passed his exam. If he passes, then you will inform the rail staff as it is unfair on everyone else that he has cheated. If he fails the exam, hopefully he will have learnt a valuable lesson and he won't cheat again.

C. As soon as the examination is complete, you would approach the exam staff and inform them that your colleague was cheating.

D. Raise your hand and wait for the rail staff to come over before informing them that your colleague is cheating. The Rail Industry requires its staff to be fully conversant and competent with all training and procedures. Cheating could put lives in danger and it is your responsibility to inform the staff.

ANSWER OPTIONS IN ORDER OF PRIORITY

1st	
2nd	
3rd	
4th	

QUESTION 20

> You are the driver of a passenger train which has Overhead Line Equipment (OLE). You have stopped at a red stop signal when you notice a person lying on the ground up ahead, immediately adjacent to, and within 2 metres of, the live OLE equipment. The person appears to be conscious and waving for help. What would you do?

ANSWER OPTIONS

A. Immediately leave the cab and approach the person safely before pulling them away from the live OLE. Once they were away from the live OLE you would inform the signaller, ECO and the Rail Safety Centre so that an ambulance could be called. Although you might get electrocuted and killed, surely it's worth the risk to save someone's life.

B. Under no circumstances would you leave the cab and approach the person to move them away from the live OLE. Instead, you would follow your training and immediately inform the signaller, the ECO and the Rail Safety Centre before continuing with your journey once the signals allowed you to do so.

C. Because the person is waving, and because they are not lying over the track, you would assume they are OK. You would continue with your journey once the signals allowed you to do so. Once on your way, you would inform the signaller and emergency services so that a rescue can be performed.

D. Under no circumstances would you leave the cab and approach the person to move them away from the live OLE. Instead, you would follow your training and immediately inform the signaller, the ECO and the Rail Safety Centre before waiting further instructions on what to do next.

TEST 1 (Train Driver related)

ANSWER OPTIONS IN ORDER OF PRIORITY

1st	
2nd	
3rd	
4th	

TRAIN DRIVER SITUATIONAL JUDGEMENT TESTS

QUESTION 21

You are the driver of a passenger train and you have just left Maidstone Station. On your journey, you start to smell something burning. You have no idea where it is coming from, or how bad it is. What would you do next?

ANSWER OPTIONS

A. Continue on with the rest of your journey. It's probably nothing serious.

B. Continue to the next station and inform the train conductor of your concerns. Ask him whether he can smell burning, and if not, then you can continue with your journey.

C. Come to a safe stop and inform the Rail Safety Centre of your concerns. If it has something to do with the engine, they will need to send out for someone to fix it immediately. You will not continue with the journey until you are told that it is safe to do so.

D. Come to a safe stop and get out of the train cab and have a look to see if you can see anything or smell the burning. If it's coming from the outside of the train cab, it is likely to have something to do with the engine and you will need to call for help.

ANSWER OPTIONS IN ORDER OF PRIORITY

1st	
2nd	
3rd	
4th	

TEST 1 (Train Driver related)

QUESTION 22

> You are driving a train from Folkestone to Ashford when, part-way through the journey, you notice a trespasser walking alongside the track. What would you do?

ANSWER OPTIONS

A. Immediately stop the train safely before leaving the cab to approach the person in order to challenge them why they are illegally trespassing.

B. Immediately inform the signaller and/or the Operations Control whilst continuing with your journey.

C. Do nothing. It is not your responsibility to get involved with trespassers.

D. Wait until you arrived at Ashford Station before informing the signaller and/or the Operations Control.

ANSWER OPTIONS IN ORDER OF PRIORITY

1st	
2nd	
3rd	
4th	

QUESTION 23

> You are walking along Euston platform towards your train when you notice that another train pulling away from the station has a defective headlight. What would you do?

ANSWER OPTIONS

A. Immediately run after the train along the platform to see if you could catch the driver's attention to inform him/her that their headlight was defective. If you could not catch their attention, you would immediately inform the signaller or person in charge.

B. Immediately inform the signaller or, if you was unable to contact them, the person in charge.

C. Do nothing. It is not your responsibility to get involved with defective headlights unless it is your train that has the defect.

D. Immediately call the destination station the train was travelling to so that the Station Manager could inform the driver.

ANSWER OPTIONS IN ORDER OF PRIORITY

1st	
2nd	
3rd	
4th	

QUESTION 24

You are driving a train from Warrington Bank Quay to Lancaster when you notice a large cow on the opposite embankment, within the boundary fence. What would you do?

ANSWER OPTIONS

A. Immediately bring the train to a safe stop before trying to usher the cow back to the safe side of the boundary fence.

B. Immediately inform the signaller or, if you were unable to contact them, the person in charge.

C. Immediately inform the signaller and the emergency services. Once you had raised the alarm, you would follow your training and attempt to stop any trains travelling in the opposite direction by showing a red flag.

D. Immediately call the emergency services.

ANSWER OPTIONS IN ORDER OF PRIORITY

1st	
2nd	
3rd	
4th	

QUESTION 25

> You are trying to communicate a difficult safety message to the signaller whilst driving your train. The signaller is having difficulty understanding a particular word you are saying to him. What would you do?

ANSWER OPTIONS

A. Keep repeating the word until he understands.

B. Use the phonetic alphabet to say the word and ask him to repeat it back to you, once he understands.

C. Use the phonetic alphabet to say the word.

D. Move on and finish the rest of your message. Hopefully he will understand the word you were trying to tell him from the rest of the information you provide him with.

ANSWER OPTIONS IN ORDER OF PRIORITY

1st	
2nd	
3rd	
4th	

TEST 1 (Train Driver related)

QUESTION 26

You are driving a train when you notice a very small fire in the cab waste bin. What would you do?

ANSWER OPTIONS

A. Inform the signaller before stopping the train immediately. You would then safely evacuate all of the passengers or move them to carriages away from the fire. You would then attempt to tackle the fire.

B. You would try to put out the fire as per your training. However, if it becomes apparent that it is not possible to put the fire out within a few seconds, you would immediately stop the train and inform the signaller and the emergency services. You would then either move passengers to carriages away from the fire or evacuate them safely.

C. Inform the signaller and ask him/her what you should do.

D. Carry on with your journey and open the cab window. If it's a small fire, the fresh air from outside should put it out.

ANSWER OPTIONS IN ORDER OF PRIORITY

1st	
2nd	
3rd	
4th	

QUESTION 27

> Following a collision with an object on the line, what would you do?

ANSWER OPTIONS

A. You wouldn't worry about it. Trains are very heavy machinery, and a train would always come out on top in any collision.

B. You would carry on driving the train to the next station. Once there, you would carry out an inspection.

C. You would inform the signaller before stopping the train. You would then ask the signaller or the person in charge what to do next.

D. You would immediately inform the signaller before bringing the train to a safe stop. You would not move the train again until you had checked for any obvious damage that may have been caused by the collision with the object, and which might affect the train's safe movement.

ANSWER OPTIONS IN ORDER OF PRIORITY

1st	
2nd	
3rd	
4th	

QUESTION 28

> Whilst driving a train you notice heavy snow start to fall. As you progress along your journey you notice the track up ahead disappear, as it is covered in deep snow that is in excess of 8 inches above the top of the rail. What would you do?

ANSWER OPTIONS

A. You wouldn't worry about it. Trains are very heavy and they will be able to carry on along the track, regardless of how much snow there is. You would carry on at the same speed so that the train arrives at the station on time.

B. You would carry on driving the train to the next station at very slow speed. Once there, providing the track had cleared, you would carry on.

C. You would slow down and immediately inform the signaller and the Operations Control how deep the snow was, and ask them what they wanted you to do next.

D. You would immediately bring the train to a safe stop and inform both the signaller and Operations Control, so they could suspend all normal train operations. You would then await further instructions.

ANSWER OPTIONS IN ORDER OF PRIORITY

1st	
2nd	
3rd	
4th	

QUESTION 29

> It's 7:30am and you are sat in the Train Drivers' mess room waiting to start your shift as a Train Driver. One of your fellow Train Drivers informs you that he went on a large drinking session the night before and he still feels worse for wear. What would you do?

ANSWER OPTIONS

A. You wouldn't do anything about it. It's up to him to decide whether or not he feels OK to drive the train or not.

B. You would immediately bring it to the attention of your supervisory manager so that he/she could take the necessary action. It is not acceptable to drive a train whilst under the influence of alcohol.

C. You would pull him to one side and tell him that you didn't think it was a good idea that he drives the train. It would be up to him to decide what to do.

D. You would congratulate him on managing to get to work on time. If he's capable of getting to work on time safely, then he sure is capable of driving a train.

ANSWER OPTIONS IN ORDER OF PRIORITY

1st	
2nd	
3rd	
4th	

TEST 1 (Train Driver related)

QUESTION 30

> You are a qualified Train Driver and you are walking along the platform at Kings Cross Station to board your train. An elderly lady approaches you and informs you that she is having trouble walking to her train. She asks you if you wouldn't mind supporting her whilst she tries to walk to her train. What would you do?

ANSWER OPTIONS

A. You would call the Train Station Customer Services Assistant. You would request that they provide mobility assistance to help the lady get to her platform safely. You would wait with the lady until assistance arrived.

B. You would tell the lady to walk to the Customer Services desk where she could ask for mobility assistance.

C. You would politely inform the lady that you are a Train Driver and that you was not in a position to help her unfortunately.

D. You would find another member of staff and ask them if they wouldn't mind walking the lady to the Customer Services desk, where she would then be able to request mobility assistance.

ANSWER OPTIONS IN ORDER OF PRIORITY

1st	
2nd	
3rd	
4th	

QUESTION 31

> You are a qualified Train Driver and you are walking along the platform at London Victoria Station to board your train. You notice a man acting suspiciously near to a coffee shop adjacent to your platform. What would you do?

ANSWER OPTIONS

A. Immediately call the British Transport Police and inform them of the man's description, the location you last saw him and what he was doing.

B. Immediately go over to the man and challenge him on his behaviour.

C. Do nothing as it is not your responsibility to challenge anyone who acts suspiciously. The British Transport Police will take care of this and they will likely have already seen him on the station CCTV cameras.

D. Keep an eye on him and take notes on his description, his location and what he was doing that made you feel he was acting suspiciously. Then, if you saw him again at the station, you would inform the police so that they could take the relevant action necessary.

ANSWER OPTIONS IN ORDER OF PRIORITY

1st	
2nd	
3rd	
4th	

QUESTION 32

> You are currently going through your Trainee Train Driver training. It is a classroom-based day where you are learning all about the different types of rolling stock operated by the Train Operating Company. You realise that you have just failed to fully understand an important piece of information the tutor was teaching. What would you do?

ANSWER OPTIONS

A. Immediately put your hand up and inform the tutor that you don't fully understand what they have been teaching. Apologise, and ask him to explain again the information you failed to understand.

B. Ask another student, at the end of the lesson, to explain it to you.

C. Don't worry about it. If it's that important, someone will explain it to you at a later date.

D. Wait until the end of the lesson before asking the teacher to explain the information again.

ANSWER OPTIONS IN ORDER OF PRIORITY

1st	
2nd	
3rd	
4th	

QUESTION 33

> You are driving a two-carriage passenger train late at night, when all of sudden a passenger pulls the emergency stop handle. There is no train guard on-board and you are solely responsible for the train and the passengers. What would you do?

ANSWER OPTIONS

A. Immediately bring the train to a safe stop before investigating what the problem is. Once you had investigated the problem, you would inform the signaller.

B. Carry on driving to the next station. If there is an incident, such as an attack, the last thing you want to do is put yourself in danger, too.

C. Immediately bring the train to a safe stop and inform the signaller before investigating the reasons for the emergency stop handle being pulled.

D. Leave the train running and walk back down the carriage to investigate what the problem was.

ANSWER OPTIONS IN ORDER OF PRIORITY

1st	
2nd	
3rd	
4th	

QUESTION 34

> You are driving a six-carriage passenger train late at night between Preston and Chorley, when the train guard informs you that a passenger is having a heart attack. Then, all of a sudden, a passenger decides to pull the emergency stop handle. What would you do?

ANSWER OPTIONS

A. Immediately bring the train to a safe stop and inform the signaller before going to the aid of the person having a heart attack.

B. Carry on driving to the next station and inform the emergency services so they could meet the train at the next station. If you were to stop between stations, it would be much harder for the emergency services to come to the aid of the casualty.

C. Carry on driving to the next station and inform the emergency services so they could meet the train at the next station. If you were to stop between stations, it would be much harder for the emergency services to come to the aid of the casualty. Then, ask the train guard to communicate to all passengers on-board for any qualified medical person(s) who might be travelling on the train to make their way to the location of the carriage where the casualty is.

D. Leave it to the train guard to sort out. Your responsibility is to just drive the train safely.

ANSWER OPTIONS IN ORDER OF PRIORITY

1st	
2nd	
3rd	
4th	

QUESTION 35

> You are a fully qualified Train Driver who has been driving the same route for many years. Up until recently, your home life has been stable. However, you have recently split up from your long-term partner and you are having to raise your children on your own, whilst relying on members of your family to look after your children whilst you are on shift. Things are starting to get on top of you, and you are finding it increasingly difficult to concentrate at work. What would you do?

ANSWER OPTIONS

A. Train Drivers are resilient and determined. You would try to stay focused and work through this difficult period in your life. Things are bound to improve soon and your concentration will get better. Because you have been driving this route for a long time, you know it like the back of your hand.

B. You would speak to your line manager and ask to be taken off driving duties until things improved.

C. You would speak to your line manager and inform him/her about your current situation and how you are feeling. You would inform him/her that you are having difficulty concentrating and that this may affect your ability to drive the trains safely.

D. You would go and see your own doctor to get a second opinion about what you should do next.

TEST 1 (Train Driver related)

ANSWER OPTIONS IN ORDER OF PRIORITY

1st	
2nd	
3rd	
4th	

QUESTION 36

> You are thinking about applying to become a Train Driver and one of the requirements is that all applicants must live within a 45-minute commutable distance from the location you are applying for. You live 1 hour and 15 minutes away from the place of work stated in the advert. What would you do?

ANSWER OPTIONS

A. You would not apply.

B. You would still apply. 30 minutes outside of the commutable distance is not that much and hopefully the train recruitment staff will understand this.

C. You would move closer to the place of work advertised and then apply.

D. You would state on the application form that you live within 45-minutes of the place of work. Then, if you were successful, you would move to be within the 45-minute distance.

ANSWER OPTIONS IN ORDER OF PRIORITY

1st	
2nd	
3rd	
4th	

TEST 1 (Train Driver related)

QUESTION 37

You have recently qualified as a Train Driver when you realise that your eyesight has started to deteriorate quickly. You have no obvious explanation as to why this health issue has started to occur. What would you do?

ANSWER OPTIONS

A. Carry on as normal for a few weeks and assess whether it gets worse or not. Sometimes these things can pass. If it continues to get worse, you would book to see your doctor.

B. You would look to change your diet and aim to eat five portions of fruit and vegetables a day. You understand that if you eat healthily, this can have a positive impact on eyesight and health in general.

C. Immediately inform your line manager of the issue and book to see your doctor to get an assessment and health check. There are strict rules regarding eyesight requirements for Train Drivers and the last thing you want to do is drive the train when unfit to do so.

D. Immediately book to see your doctor to get a full health check and assessment. He would then sign you off sick if he felt you were not fit for duty as a Train Driver.

ANSWER OPTIONS IN ORDER OF PRIORITY

1st	
2nd	
3rd	
4th	

QUESTION 38

> You are driving a train late at night from London Victoria to Maidstone when the train guard informs you via the communication system that a fight has broken out in one of the carriages. She tells you the fight is between two drunken men who are refusing to stop. She also tells you that there are parents and children in the carriage where the fight is taking place. What would you do?

ANSWER OPTIONS

A. Ask the train guard to deal with the situation and keep you informed.

B. Immediately request that British Transport Police meet the train at the next station so they can deal with the incident.

C. Immediately request that British Transport Police meet the train at the next station so they can deal with the incident. Then, in order to ensure the safety of all passengers, ask the train guard to move everyone not involved with the incident to a different carriage.

D. Immediately stop the train and inform the signaller of your location. Then, request the attendance of the British Transport Police.

ANSWER OPTIONS IN ORDER OF PRIORITY

1st	
2nd	
3rd	
4th	

TEST 1 (Train Driver related)

QUESTION 39

> You have just completed a long shift as a Train Driver and you are walking to your car to start your journey home. All of a sudden you realise that you forgot to inform the next Train Driver, who will be using the train you last drove, about a non-safety critical defect. What would you?

ANSWER OPTIONS

A. Make your way back to the train station and inform the driver of the defect. Safety is paramount, and even though the defect is non-safety critical, it is still important you inform him.

B. Because it is non-safety critical, it is not essential that you inform him. You have had a long day at work and you are now off duty. You would continue home.

C. Because it is non-safety critical, it is not essential that you inform him straight away. You have had a long day at work and you are now off duty. You would continue home and make sure you call him as soon as you get home to inform him of the defect.

D. Make your way back to the train station and inform the driver of the defect. Safety is paramount, and even though the defect is non-safety critical, it is still important you inform him. You would then ensure that any future defects were handed over to the driver before you went off shift.

ANSWER OPTIONS IN ORDER OF PRIORITY

1st	
2nd	
3rd	
4th	

QUESTION 40

A bridge is reported to have been hit by a lorry on the railway line on which you are travelling. The signaller tells you of the location of the bridge and informs you not to travel above 5km/h until the length of the train has passed through the bridge. Unfortunately, by travelling at 5km/h this will make the train excessively late for your arrival at the next station. What would you do?

ANSWER OPTIONS

A. You would follow the instructions of the signaller and not proceed above 5km/h.

B. You would inform the signaller that, by travelling under 5km/h, this would make your train arrive late at the next station.

C. You would ignore the speed restriction and continue at the same speed to ensure you reach the station on time.

D. You would ask the train guard for a second opinion on whether you should travel above 5km/h, or stick to the signaller's instructions.

ANSWER OPTIONS IN ORDER OF PRIORITY

1st	
2nd	
3rd	
4th	

SUGGESTED ANSWERS TEST 1

SUGGESTED ANSWERS TEST 1

In this section you will find the suggested answers to the test. The reason why we have provided 'suggested answers' as opposed to definitive answers, is simply because how you react or make decisions when presented with different situations/scenarios, will be entirely different to the next person. As stated at the start of this guide, it is important you answer the questions honestly, based on how you would react in the given situation. The suggested answers provided here are how we would respond in the given situation/scenario.

SUGGESTED ANSWERS IN ORDER OF PRIORITY

QUESTION 1

A
D
C
B

QUESTION 2

B
D
C
A

QUESTION 3

D
A
C
B

SUGGESTED ANSWERS TEST 1

QUESTION 4

A
C
B
D

QUESTION 5

A
D
B
C

QUESTION 6

C
D
B
A

QUESTION 7

C
B
A
D

QUESTION 8

C
D
B
A

QUESTION 9

B

C

D

A

QUESTION 10

A

C

B

D

QUESTION 11

A

C

D

B

QUESTION 12

D

C

B

A

QUESTION 13

C

D

A

B

SUGGESTED ANSWERS TEST 1

QUESTION 14

A
B
C
D

QUESTION 15

D
C
B
A

QUESTION 16

A
C
D
B

QUESTION 17

B
A
D
C

QUESTION 18

A
D
B
C

QUESTION 19

D

C

B

A

QUESTION 20

D

B

C

A

QUESTION 21

C

D

B

A

QUESTION 22

B

D

A

C

QUESTION 23

B

A

D

C

SUGGESTED ANSWERS TEST 1

QUESTION 24

C

B

D

A

QUESTION 25

B

C

A

D

QUESTION 26

B

A

C

D

QUESTION 27

D

C

B

A

QUESTION 28

D

C

B

A

QUESTION 29

B

C

A

D

QUESTION 30

A

D

B

C

QUESTION 31

A

B

D

C

QUESTION 32

A

D

B

C

QUESTION 33

C

A

B

D

SUGGESTED ANSWERS TEST 1

QUESTION 34

C

B

A

D

QUESTION 35

C

B

D

A

QUESTION 36

C

D

B

A

QUESTION 37

C

D

B

A

QUESTION 38

C

B

D

A

QUESTION 39

D

A

C

B

QUESTION 40

A

B

D

C

Now that you have completed test number 1, please move on to test 2, which consists of non-Train Driver related situational judgement questions.

TEST 2

(Non Train Driver related)

TEST 2 (NON TRAIN DRIVER RELATED)

In this next section of the guide we are going to look at an entirely different format of situational judgement test: ones that are non Train Driver related. It is great practice to try as many different types of situational judgement tests as possible, to ensure that you are fully prepared for your Train Driver assessment.

You will notice that, following each question, you are asked to indicate which of the presented answer options (A, B, C or D) is:

- Very helpful
- Helpful
- Neither helpful nor unhelpful
- Unhelpful
- Very unhelpful

You will notice that there are 5 options to choose from, yet only 4 answer options. That means, therefore, one of the 5 options will be left blank.

Take a look at the sample question below:

SAMPLE QUESTION

You are working at a local fast food restaurant. During a busy shift, you are paired with a new staff member on the fry station. In his panic to get food out on time, the new staff member takes a hot basket of fries and accidentally hits you in the arm with them. The grease basket badly sears the skin of your forearm. How do you react?

A. Ask a senior staff member to take over, whilst you go and receive medical treatment.

B. Man up and get back to work.

C. Yell at the new staff member, and refuse to work with him anymore.

D. Leave the new staff member in charge of the fry station and report the incident to your manager.

TEST 2 (Non Train Driver related)

SUGGESTED ANSWERS

Very helpful – A

Helpful –

Neither helpful nor unhelpful – D

Unhelpful – C

Very unhelpful – B

Explanation to the answers:

A. Ask a senior staff member to take over, whilst you go and receive medical treatment.

This is **very helpful** because it ensures that the fry station won't crash whilst you are receiving treatment, and ensures that you receive medical attention for your injury.

D. Leave the new staff member in charge of the fry station, report the incident to your manager.

This is **neither helpful nor unhelpful**. While you are receiving medical attention/reporting the incident, you are also leaving someone inexperienced and potentially incapable in charge of what should be a two-person job.

C. Yell at the new staff member, and refuse to work with him anymore.

This is **unhelpful**. It shows a lack of professionalism and a refusal to accept that 'mistakes happen'.

B. Man up and get back to work.

This is **very unhelpful**. By working with a severe injury, you are breaking health and safety rules and regulations, and this could lead to further damage.

Now that you understand how this type of situational judgement test works, work through the 40 sample questions that follow. You have 40 minutes to complete this test. The suggested answers are provided at the end of the test.

TRAIN DRIVER SITUATIONAL JUDGEMENT TESTS

QUESTION 1

> You are working in an office when a member of staff, who is in a wheelchair, approaches you. She asks you if you would be willing to swap desks, as your desk is closer to the exit route, and it will make it easier for her to go to the toilet when required. How do you react?

A. Say no. You are already settled in at your desk and to move would cause unnecessary upheaval.

B. Say yes. This is not a problem for you and you can see why moving desks would help her out and improve her working day.

C. Tell her to speak to your boss first, to see if he is in agreement with her request. If he doesn't have a problem with it, neither do you.

D. Tell her you would be willing to swap desks providing she is prepared to move all of your belongings to the new desk.

ANSWER OPTIONS

Very helpful	
Helpful	
Neither helpful nor unhelpful	
Unhelpful	
Very unhelpful	

QUESTION 2

> You are a train conductor working on your local line. At 10 past 10 in the morning, you are performing your hourly ticket inspection. You come across a man on the train who has not purchased a ticket. He claims that the reason for this is because he had to board the train quickly. It's an emergency as his mother has taken a fall and is in hospital. He has the money to pay the fare there and then. His station is two stops away. What do you do?

A. Consult with the other people in the carriage as to what to do.

B. Allow him to pay the full ticket fare to his intended stop.

C. Perform a citizen's arrest. This man is a criminal.

D. Kick him off at the next stop. The rules state that if he hasn't paid, then he must leave the train.

ANSWER OPTIONS

Very helpful	
Helpful	
Neither helpful nor unhelpful	
Unhelpful	
Very unhelpful	

QUESTION 3

Your company has recently hired a new staff member. He has only been working for you for 2 days, but you have noticed him making inappropriate remarks towards female staff members. Your manager does not seem to have noticed. One of your female colleagues has confessed that his behaviour makes her feel uncomfortable, but she does not want to risk jeopardising the employee's future, especially since he has only just joined the company. Another female staff member claims that the next time he does it, she will 'give him a smack'. What do you do?

A. Take the new employee to one side and tell him that his behaviour needs to change.

B. Go to your manager and explain the situation.

C. Encourage your female colleagues to speak to your manager.

D. Ignore the behaviour. He's only joking.

ANSWER OPTIONS

Very helpful	
Helpful	
Neither helpful nor unhelpful	
Unhelpful	
Very unhelpful	

QUESTION 4

You have been working in a hugely successful company for the past 10 years. Recently, however, your company's fortunes seem to have taken a turn for the worse. Profits are at an all-time low, employees seem to be drastically underperforming and your sales manager refuses to accept any of the blame. He claims that the bad results are out of his control, and that the products being produced are simply of poor quality. Privately, he has also informed you that he believes customers are being scared off by current employee sales techniques, and as a result won't purchase from the organisation. During a recent team meeting, one of your colleagues tried to raise her concerns. Your sales manager lambasted her, branding her weak and naïve. Your colleague was extremely upset by this behaviour, and is considering making a complaint of sexism to the chairman of the company. Although in your opinion there is no evidence to suggest this, she has asked you to act as a witness to her statement. What do you do?

A. Agree to act as a witness, but tell the chairman that there is no evidence to suggest sexism.

B. Tell the chairman that you believe your sales manager was acting in a sexist manner.

C. Agree to act a witness. Tell the chairman that you believe your sales manager is out of his depth, and that you would be better suited for his job.

D. Encourage your colleague to sue the company. Sexism is unacceptable.

ANSWER OPTIONS

Very helpful	
Helpful	
Neither helpful nor unhelpful	
Unhelpful	
Very unhelpful	

QUESTION 5

> You are working for a train company as a platform assistant. Part of your job is to assist disabled passengers on and off the train. It is the middle of a weekday, and therefore there are very few customers to deal with. On the other side of the platform, you notice a well-known celebrity. One of your colleagues has noticed this too, and suggests that you both go over to the other side to get her autograph. What do you do?

A. Agree to cross over and get an autograph. This could be your only chance to meet such a prestigious person.

B. Tell your colleague that you won't be going anywhere. What they do is up to them.

C. Refuse to go, and encourage your colleague to do the same. This would be unprofessional.

D. Take mobile pictures of the celebrity and post it on Twitter.

ANSWER OPTIONS

Very helpful	
Helpful	
Neither helpful nor unhelpful	
Unhelpful	
Very unhelpful	

TEST 2 (Non Train Driver related)

QUESTION 6

You are working on a train platform when two passengers get off the train. They appear to be arguing furiously. One of the men approaches you, claiming that the other man took his bag. The other man says that the bag was his all along, and that the first man is lying. He states 'finder's keepers'. You ask the man to hand over the bag to you, so that the CCTV footage on the train can be reviewed. This leaves the first man irate. As you turn around to deal with him, the second man runs off with the bag, jumps into a taxi, and is gone. What do you do?

A. Offer to take the man's contact details, so that he can be reimbursed for a portion of his fare.

B. Tell the man there is nothing that can be done.

C. Report the incident to senior station management. Tell the man that your company will be in touch.

D. Take the man into a private room where you can write up a report of the incident, which will then be passed on to the police.

ANSWER OPTIONS

Very helpful	
Helpful	
Neither helpful nor unhelpful	
Unhelpful	
Very unhelpful	

QUESTION 7

> You are working as a train conductor. Every Tuesday, you conduct the 10 past 10 train from Ficshire East to Ficshire West. There is a man who boards your train every Tuesday. You have noticed that he wears a wedding ring. He sits in the same carriage in the same seat every time. The man often brings female companions on the train with him, and appears very affectionate to all of them. In the past 2 months, you have seen the man kiss at least 5 different women. You suspect him of cheating. What do you do?

A. Ignore the situation. It's none of your business.

B. Confront the man on the spot. Cheating is immoral.

C. Take the man to one side and quietly ask him to explain his behaviour.

D. Ask the man for some dating advice.

ANSWER OPTIONS

Very helpful	
Helpful	
Neither helpful nor unhelpful	
Unhelpful	
Very unhelpful	

TEST 2 (Non Train Driver related) 83

QUESTION 8

> You are the centre manager for a well-known writing retreat in the English countryside. Part of your role is ensuring that the centre is well staffed, food goes out on time and that the centre is kept clean and tidy. You have recently taken on a new staff member, who is struggling with his position. Today you have discovered that the new staff member has forgotten to pre-order food supplies, meaning that there is no way to cook dinner for the course attendees that evening. The staff member is fairly upset at his mistake. What do you say to him?

A. 'Pack your bags. You're sacked.'

B. 'Mistakes happen. Let's pull the team together and brainstorm some ideas as to how we can fix this.'

C. 'Maybe you should consider whether this is the right position for you.'

D. 'I'd like you to apologise personally to the course attendees. You should explain the situation, and whose fault it is.'

ANSWER OPTIONS

Very helpful	
Helpful	
Neither helpful nor unhelpful	
Unhelpful	
Very unhelpful	

QUESTION 9

> You are the manager of a major sporting retail store. The previous day, one of your staff members was using a ladder to retrieve an item for a customer. Due to incorrect safety precautions, the ladder fell, injuring the staff member. She has broken her ankle, and therefore won't be in work for a significant period of time. It is your job to call her the next day. What do you say to her?

A. 'Hi. I'm really sorry about the incident that occurred yesterday. We hope to see you back at work soon.'

B. 'Hi. Unfortunately, since you are part time, and can no longer work, we are going to have to terminate your contract.'

C. 'Hi. Do you think you could come in and work on crutches?'

D. 'Hi. Do you think you could ring around and find someone else to cover your hours whilst you are off sick?'

ANSWER OPTIONS

Very helpful	
Helpful	
Neither helpful nor unhelpful	
Unhelpful	
Very unhelpful	

QUESTION 10

> You are a staff member at a care home. You recently took a week off for a relative's funeral. Upon your return to the care home, you hear that your manager has been gossiping about you behind your back, with the other staff at the care home. According to your source, your manager questioned the necessity of taking 5 days off for a funeral, and called you lazy. You are upset by these claims. What do you do?

A – Spread bad rumours about your manager. Two can play that game.

B – Take your manager to one side and question her on whether the claims are true. Explain why you needed the time off.

C – Arrange a team meeting to try to get to the bottom of this.

D – Ring your manager in your own time to try and discuss the situation further.

ANSWER OPTIONS

Very helpful	
Helpful	
Neither helpful nor unhelpful	
Unhelpful	
Very unhelpful	

QUESTION 11

> You are working as a shop assistant in a toy shop. A woman approaches you and asks for help locating a particular brand of toy. She informs you that the toy is showing 'IN STOCK' on the company website and that she has travelled 10 miles to buy it. After searching for 10 minutes you establish that the toy is out of stock and the information on the website is incorrect. What would you do?

A. Apologise to the customer and say you are sorry but there is nothing more you can do.

B. Apologise to the customer and inform her that there is another toy shop 15 miles away in the next town. If she travels there, they might have the toy she wants in stock.

C. Apologise unreservedly for the toy not being in stock. Tell her that you will order the toy immediately from your supplier and then deliver it to her home as soon as it arrives. She will not be charged for either the toy or the delivery due to the inconvenience and stress caused.

D. Apologise unreservedly for the toy not being in stock. Tell her that you will order the toy immediately from your supplier and then deliver it to her home as soon as it arrives. She will be charged for the toy, but not for the delivery, due to the inconvenience and stress caused.

ANSWER OPTIONS

Very helpful	
Helpful	
Neither helpful nor unhelpful	
Unhelpful	
Very unhelpful	

QUESTION 12

> You are working as a delivery driver for a well-known supermarket delivering food to customers' homes. Whilst attending someone's home to deliver their food order, they offer you £10 as a thank you for being prompt and for giving an excellent service. The company has a strict policy which states that you must not take any form of tip or financial reward from customers whilst at work. What would you do?

A. Thank them for the money, put it in your pocket, and leave a happy person. Nobody will ever know that you took the money, so there's no harm.

B. Thank them for the money, but explain that you are unable to accept tips or financial rewards of this nature. Tell them that if they would like to give a reward, the supermarket supports local charities and they will be able to donate via their website.

C. Thank them for their kind offer, but explain that you are unable to accept tips or financial rewards of this nature.

D. Walk away and ignore them.

ANSWER OPTIONS

Very helpful	
Helpful	
Neither helpful nor unhelpful	
Unhelpful	
Very unhelpful	

QUESTION 13

> You are working as a Health and Safety assessor and are visiting a local warehouse to talk to the staff about risk assessments. Whilst walking around the warehouse you notice that a number of the fire doors are wedged open illegally. What do you do?

A. Ignore it. You are at the premise to talk to the staff about a specific subject and it would be inappropriate to say anything there and then.

B. Remove the wedges yourself and then report the situation to the local Fire Safety Officer when you return to your office later that day. He/she can then carry out a formal inspection.

C. Inform the responsible person at the warehouse that the wedges need to be moved immediately. Then, once you return to the office you will report the matter to your local Fire Safety Officer so that he/she can carry out a thorough inspection of the premise.

D. Remove the wedges holding the doors open yourself and say nothing more about it.

ANSWER OPTIONS

Very helpful	
Helpful	
Neither helpful nor unhelpful	
Unhelpful	
Very unhelpful	

QUESTION 14

> During an office meeting your line manager is explaining a number of changes that are being introduced to the working day. These changes will mean that you and your work colleagues will have more tasks to complete during the working day. The majority of other members of the team start to make their objections to the changes heard. What would you do?

A. Join in with the objections. Why change things when everything is going OK as it is?

B. Keep your head down. Whilst you don't agree with the changes you don't want to get into trouble for raising your concerns.

C. Accept the changes yourself. It doesn't matter what the others think. After all, they are entitled to their own opinion.

D. Accept the changes. Change is part of working life. You would also try and explain the benefit of the changes to those who are sceptical.

ANSWER OPTIONS

Very helpful	
Helpful	
Neither helpful nor unhelpful	
Unhelpful	
Very unhelpful	

QUESTION 15

> You are working as a bus driver and it is coming to the end of your shift. In 5 minutes' time, you are due to sign off and head home. Your line manager approaches you and asks you to mop the bus depot floor before you go off duty. You realise that this will take you 15 minutes to do the job professionally. What would you do?

A. Carry out the task as requested professionally, even though it will mean that you have to stay behind at work for an additional 10 minutes.

B. Inform your manager that you are going off duty in 5 minutes' time and that you won't be able to do the task to the required standard. Ask her if there is anyone else who can do the task.

C. Carry out the task to a slightly lesser standard, therefore finishing your shift on time.

D. Politely refuse to carry out the task.

ANSWER OPTIONS

Very helpful	
Helpful	
Neither helpful nor unhelpful	
Unhelpful	
Very unhelpful	

QUESTION 16

> You are managing a team of six people at a distribution centre. It is approaching the annual peak time for business where your staff will need to be at their best in order to cope with demand. You are concerned as all of your staff have been making careless mistakes whilst dispatching goods, due to increased workload. What would you do?

A. Get the team together and tell them that, if matters do not improve, you will speak to the main boss about getting them replaced.

B. Hold a team meeting as soon as possible to establish the reasons why so many mistakes are being made. Then, formulate and agree a plan with all of the team in order to improve performance.

C. Get stuck in yourself more to help the team out. Clearly they are very busy and they could do with an extra pair of hands.

D. Speak to your boss and explain to her that you need to take on another member of staff to ease the pressure on the team.

ANSWER OPTIONS

Very helpful	
Helpful	
Neither helpful nor unhelpful	
Unhelpful	
Very unhelpful	

QUESTION 17

> You are working as a retail assistant in a high street store. It is a very busy day in the shop and everyone is working flat out serving and helping customers. You are walking towards the back of the shop through the storage area to take your 10 minute tea break, when you notice that the contents of a large shelf have all fallen on the floor. You estimate it would take you at least 10 minutes to put all of the contents back on the shelf. What would you do?

A. Walk around the contents and go for your tea break. You are legally entitled to a break and someone else will be able to clear up the mess.

B. Inform your manager that you are going to put the contents back on the shelf and request that you take your 10 minute tea break after the job is complete.

C. Inform your manager that the contents have fallen on the floor and ask him if he can find someone else to put the contents back on the shelf as you are about to go on your tea break.

D. Forget about your tea break and put the contents back on the shelf yourself.

ANSWER OPTIONS

Very helpful	
Helpful	
Neither helpful nor unhelpful	
Unhelpful	
Very unhelpful	

QUESTION 18

> You are working alone as a barista at a local coffee shop. It is a Saturday morning and there is a large queue of people waiting to be served. All of a sudden the coffee machine breaks down and you will be unable to serve coffee for the rest of the day. You will still be able to serve soft drinks and tea. What would you do?

A. Apologise to the people in the queue and inform them you will not be able to serve them due to the breakdown of the coffee machine, which is beyond your control. Then, close the shop and make your way home.

B. Apologise to the people in the queue and inform them that you will only be able to serve soft drinks and tea due to the breakdown of the coffee machine. Then, create a sign that says 'COFFEE MACHINE BROKEN – WE ARE ONLY ABLE TO SERVE SOFT DRINKS AND TEA – APOLOGIES FOR ANY INCONVENIENCE CAUSED' and place it on the shop door so that people can make a decision whether or not they want to come in.

C. Apologise to each person as they reach the front of the queue and explain to them that you are unable to serve coffee but that you can serve them soft drinks or tea.

D. Call your boss and ask her what she wants you to do.

ANSWER OPTIONS

Very helpful	
Helpful	
Neither helpful nor unhelpful	
Unhelpful	
Very unhelpful	

QUESTION 19

> You are a supervisor for a small business and you have been carrying out interviews for a new role within the company. You interviewed 4 people for the new role and one of them has been successful. After you write rejection letters to the 3 candidates who were unsuccessful, one of them arrives at your office to complain. He says he is bitterly disappointed in the fact he was not successful and wants an explanation from you. What would you do?

A. Tell him you are not obliged to go into reasons why he was not successful and ask him to leave.

B. Tell him that, although he was not successful this time, you will consider him for any future jobs that come up at the company.

C. Listen to his concerns and allow him to vent his frustrations. Once he has finished, explain to him that there is a robust and thorough selection process in place and that unfortunately, on this occasion, he was unsuccessful and that someone else was found more suitable for the role. Then, offer him constructive feedback on his performance during the interview.

D. Invite him to sit down and make him a cup of tea. Whilst you are out of the office, call your boss and ask for advice on how to deal with the situation.

ANSWER OPTIONS

Very helpful	
Helpful	
Neither helpful nor unhelpful	
Unhelpful	
Very unhelpful	

TEST 2 (Non Train Driver related)

QUESTION 20

> You are working as a retail shop assistant and it is your turn to work on the customer services desk. A man, who appears to be angry, approaches you with an electric shaver in his hand. He tells you that he only bought the shaver from your shop three weeks ago but that it has now stopped working completely. He wants a replacement to be provided. The shop has a 28-day refund/exchange policy providing a receipt can be supplied. He does not have a receipt. What would you do?

A. Apologise for the inconvenience that has been caused through the defective shaver. Explain to the customer the companies refund policy and that a receipt is required for a refund or exchange. However, explain to him that, if he can provide proof of purchase, by way of a card statement, that you will ask your manager if you can exchange the shaver for him.

B. Explain to him that, because he does not have a receipt, you are not able to help him.

C. Apologise for the inconvenience that has been caused through the defective shaver and then happily exchange the defective shaver for a new one.

D. Ask your manager what he thinks you should do.

ANSWER OPTIONS

Very helpful	
Helpful	
Neither helpful nor unhelpful	
Unhelpful	
Very unhelpful	

TRAIN DRIVER SITUATIONAL JUDGEMENT TESTS

QUESTION 21

> You are a supervisor working for a large corporate organisation. You are in a meeting with your manager along with ten other supervisors. Your manager has a very strong accent different to your own and tends to talk quickly, often making it difficult for people to understand her. So far, during the meeting, you have not been able to understand most of what she has been saying. What would you do?

A. As soon as there becomes a natural break in her talk, raise your hand and explain that you are finding it difficult to understand most of what she is saying. Respectfully ask if she would please slow down so that you can take in all of the important information she is relaying.

B. Wait to the end of the meeting before speaking to her in private and explain to her that you didn't understand most of what she was saying.

C. Do nothing.

D. Wait until the end of the meeting and then ask your work colleagues for clarification on what she was saying.

ANSWER OPTIONS

Very helpful	
Helpful	
Neither helpful nor unhelpful	
Unhelpful	
Very unhelpful	

QUESTION 22

> You have just started a new job as a manager with a large corporate company. On your first day at work another manager approaches you and starts telling you negative things about your boss. She tells you that he is very poor at doing his job and that you shouldn't trust him as he tends to speak about his staff behind their backs. What would you do?

A. Challenge her in a respectable manner and say that you think she is wrong for saying these things about a senior member of the team.

B. Thank her for the information and be on your guard from now on when dealing with your manager.

C. Thank her for the information but explain that you do not want to pre-judge people and you want to have an entirely open mind. You will take him as you find him.

D. Thank her for the information and then ask other people within the organisation if they have had the same experience whilst working with your manager.

ANSWER OPTIONS

Very helpful	
Helpful	
Neither helpful nor unhelpful	
Unhelpful	
Very unhelpful	

TRAIN DRIVER SITUATIONAL JUDGEMENT TESTS

QUESTION 23

> You are a manager of a hotel chain and you receive a call from your managing director at head office. She has requested that you spend the day managing at another hotel twenty-five miles away as the current manager there has gone off sick. You have a large amount of paperwork to catch up on and you intended on doing it today whilst working at your own hotel. What would you do?

A. Explain that you cannot meet their request as you have lots of paperwork to catch up on.

B. Explain to head office that you have lots of paperwork to catch up on and ask them how they want you to prioritise your work.

C. Tell head office that you have lots of paperwork to catch up on but that you are prepared to ring around the other hotels in the region to see if there is another manager available to go to the hotel. If not, then you would be prepared to go and you would have to catch up with your paperwork another time.

D. Agree to go to the hotel for the rest of the day and take your paperwork with you to do, whilst you are there.

ANSWER OPTIONS

Very helpful	
Helpful	
Neither helpful nor unhelpful	
Unhelpful	
Very unhelpful	

TEST 2 (Non Train Driver related)

QUESTION 24

> You are working as an admin assistant in a typical office environment when you can't help overhearing your manager reprimanding one of your work colleagues for poor performance. Your manager is clearly not happy with your colleague and he is making it perfectly clear that he expects to see rapid improvement. You are concerned for your work colleague as he hasn't been himself lately and you can see that something has been troubling him. What would you do?

A. Speak to your colleague in private and ask him whether anything is wrong. You would also offer your support to see if you can help him through this difficult period he is going through.

B. Approach your manager in confidence and tell him that you think there might be something wrong with your work colleague, which is ultimately having an impact on his work performance.

C. Do nothing. You do not want to interfere as it is not your problem.

D. Speak to your work colleague and offer to do some of his work for him in order to ease the pressure he is under from his manager.

ANSWER OPTIONS

Very helpful	
Helpful	
Neither helpful nor unhelpful	
Unhelpful	
Very unhelpful	

QUESTION 25

> You are a supervisor working in a warehouse and it is 30 minutes until your shift ends. The oncoming shift supervisor calls you and tells you he is going to be 30 minutes late as he is stuck in traffic. You have a dinner date booked with your girlfriend that evening and you need to get away. What would you do?

A. Tell the oncoming shift workers that they will have to work on their own, unsupervised, for 30 minutes until their supervisor arrives.

B. Call your girlfriend and tell her you will be late coming home. Then, supervise the oncoming shift workers until their supervisor arrives.

C. Call your boss and ask her what she thinks you should do.

D. Leave at the end of your shift. The fact that he is going to be late is not your problem.

ANSWER OPTIONS

Very helpful	
Helpful	
Neither helpful nor unhelpful	
Unhelpful	
Very unhelpful	

QUESTION 26

> You have been working in a new team for 3 months now. When you started, your line manager put you on a 6-month development programme where you would be closely supervised for that period of time. You now feel very much ready to work alone and the close supervision is starting to frustrate you and hinder your development. What would you do?

A. Complete the 6-month supervision period as planned and not say anything about how you feel.

B. Tell your work colleagues how you feel and get their advice on what they think you should do.

C. Start working more on your own without telling anyone.

D. Arrange a meeting with your line manager to explain how you now feel ready to work more on your own, unsupervised. Ask for his permission for the supervision period to come to an end.

ANSWER OPTIONS

Very helpful	
Helpful	
Neither helpful nor unhelpful	
Unhelpful	
Very unhelpful	

QUESTION 27

> You are the supervisor of a small team working for an online mail order company. It is December and it's the busiest time of the year. Your team is snowed under with work and some of the team members are clearly feeling the strain. You have a team development meeting booked for the forthcoming Tuesday morning. However, one of the team members approaches you and tells you that she won't be at the meeting as she is too busy to attend. What would you do?

A. Spend time with the team member to identify ways in which she can manage her time more efficiently so that she can attend the team development meeting.

B. Tell the team member that the team development meeting is mandatory. She must attend.

C. Tell the team member that you understand how she is feeling and that she does not need to attend the team development meeting.

D. Get a member of staff from another team to cover the team member's workload during the day of the meeting so that she can attend.

ANSWER OPTIONS

Very helpful	
Helpful	
Neither helpful nor unhelpful	
Unhelpful	
Very unhelpful	

QUESTION 28

> You have noticed one of your colleagues continuously turning up to work with a hangover. You haven't said anything before, but you've realised that the situation is becoming more frequent. Today at work, the same colleague has turned up to work, and you can smell alcohol on their breath. The colleague is disruptive, loud, and is clearly still intoxicated. What would you do?

A. You tell your colleague that he is being extremely unprofessional and tell him to arrange a lift home and sober up.

B. You inform your colleague that you are aware of the said issue, and that he should seek help.

C. You get another one of your colleagues to drive him home, so you can continue working in peace.

D. You tell him to make a cup of coffee and sober up, and get on with his work quietly.

ANSWER OPTIONS

Very helpful	
Helpful	
Neither helpful nor unhelpful	
Unhelpful	
Very unhelpful	

QUESTION 29

> You are the project manager of a team of 5. Your group has been tasked with analysing and correlating key intelligence information which has been passed on to you by another sector, before sending it off to management. Halfway through the project, one of your team members approaches you, claiming that she no longer wants to work with another member of the team. The reason for this is that she believes the person in question has been undermining her and making sarcastic comments directed at her. You have not heard anything of this sort. The individual threatening to leave the team is highly experienced and her absence would severely damage the group's chances of success. What would you do?

A. Explain to your team member that the group need her, and that she should rise above it and continue with the project.

B. Wait to see if you hear anything as mentioned by the individual, and then take action.

C. Sit the individual in question down, and ask their side of the story.

D. Sit them both down to try and resolve the issue, before continuing on with the project.

ANSWER OPTIONS

Very helpful	
Helpful	
Neither helpful nor unhelpful	
Unhelpful	
Very unhelpful	

QUESTION 30

> You have just finished creating an important presentation that is being presented this afternoon. You show it to your boss and ask for their feedback. Whilst he says he is impressed with the overall layout and design of the presentation, he has a few concerns. He feels as though the presentation is lacking in statistics and financial data, which is crucial to this presentation's success. You know that adding this information is going to take time, and you are not sure if you have enough research to go on to add this information in such short notice. What would you do?

A. Explain to your boss that the presentation is being presented that afternoon, and you do not have enough time to add in that information.

B. Inform your boss that whilst you cannot add in this information due to time constraints, you will be happy to answer any questions they have.

C. Ignore your boss' concerns and present the presentation the way it is.

D. Ask your colleagues to help you with the additional information, so that you can ensure the work gets added.

ANSWER OPTIONS

Very helpful	
Helpful	
Neither helpful nor unhelpful	
Unhelpful	
Very unhelpful	

QUESTION 31

> You are working as an administrative assistant for a local company. The Human Resources department has sent an email round to everyone in your department advising you all to use up any holiday leave time during this quiet period. However, your line manager has seen this email and he seems less than impressed. What would you do?

A. Take the vacation days as advised by the Human Resources department.

B. Decide not to take your vacation days if it is going to upset the boss.

C. Negotiate your time off with your boss and reiterate that you are allowed said number of days off.

D. Discuss with your boss the importance of employment contracts, which reiterate the number of vacation days an employee is allowed.

ANSWER OPTIONS

Very helpful	
Helpful	
Neither helpful nor unhelpful	
Unhelpful	
Very unhelpful	

QUESTION 32

> You have been at your job for nearly 3 years now, and you and the Managing Director have become good friends. However, you have noticed that the Managing Director has a very different attitude towards some of your colleagues. On numerous occasions, you have noticed him making sarcastic comments, and acting in a rude and unprofessional manner. You overheard your colleagues moaning about this to one another, and you feel that you need to do something before the situation escalates. What would you do?

A. Try to talk to your colleagues about the situation and show that you understand how they must be feeling.

B. Continue being good friends with the Managing Director and not say anything to him. He is a clever man, and will soon realise that his behaviour is unacceptable.

C. Bring up this issue in a polite conversation with your Managing Director, and voice what your colleagues are feeling.

D. Ignore what your colleagues are saying. You are in the good books, and you don't want to stir anything up that may jeopardise your position.

ANSWER OPTIONS

Very helpful	
Helpful	
Neither helpful nor unhelpful	
Unhelpful	
Very unhelpful	

QUESTION 33

> You've had a hectic day at work, and you have already worked over an hour over your normal hours. You need to finish all of your emails before you leave, and you've just sent your last one. However, as you read back through the email, you notice that you have sent the email to the wrong person. This email contains confidential client information. What would you do?

A. Send a follow-up email immediately after apologising for the mistake. Send the email to the correct person.

B. Send the email again, but this time to the correct person. The person you sent the email to will just assume it's a mistake.

C. Leave the office, and deal with the issue first thing in the morning.

D. Explain the situation to your manager, and let him deal with resolving the issue.

ANSWER OPTIONS

Very helpful	
Helpful	
Neither helpful nor unhelpful	
Unhelpful	
Very unhelpful	

QUESTION 34

> A new employee has recently started in the same department you work in. You haven't bonded with this employee much, but on the rare occasion, you notice that he often discusses his strong religious beliefs, and is trying to enforce some of his views on other people. You are not the only one who has noticed this, and you have realised that one of your colleagues has been upset by some of the things that have been discussed. What would you do?

A. Voice your opinions regarding religion and demonstrate that everyone is different.

B. Inform your new colleague how important first impressions are.

C. Comfort your colleague who has been upset by the discussion, and tell her to speak to the new colleague about this upset.

D. Bring it up in discussion at the next team meeting and ensure everyone understands how powerful topics such as religion or politics are discouraged at the working environment.

ANSWER OPTIONS

Very helpful	
Helpful	
Neither helpful nor unhelpful	
Unhelpful	
Very unhelpful	

QUESTION 35

> You have been in a relationship with one of your work colleagues for the last two years. However, you have recently decided to split from your partner. You are still working in the same department, but you notice that the work environment has become very hostile towards you. Some people have stopped talking to you altogether, and others make sly remarks. It doesn't look as though your ex is experiencing this at all. What would you do?

A. Discuss with your ex about the situation, and come to some agreement so that you can both continue to work in a comfortable environment.

B. Ask your colleagues what their problem is – it's none of their business what has happened between you and your ex.

C. Inform the Head of the Department that you are unable to work in such a hostile environment, and want to be relocated to a different department.

D. Avoid the colleagues that are making it difficult for you, and continue on with your daily routine.

ANSWER OPTIONS

Very helpful	
Helpful	
Neither helpful nor unhelpful	
Unhelpful	
Very unhelpful	

QUESTION 36

> Over the last few weeks, you have noticed that large amounts of company property have been going missing. Yesterday, you noticed one of your colleagues putting stationery in her bag. You have only seen her do this once, but you believe she must be the one responsible for the property going missing. What would you do?

A. Do nothing. You do not have enough evidence to go by, and if she is guilty, she will be found out soon.

B. Decide that you don't have enough evidence yet, so you will need to gather more evidence to catch her out.

C. Confront your colleague and inform her about company policy in regards to taking company property.

D. Inform your manager that your colleague is responsible for the large amounts of company property going missing.

ANSWER OPTIONS

Very helpful	
Helpful	
Neither helpful nor unhelpful	
Unhelpful	
Very unhelpful	

TRAIN DRIVER SITUATIONAL JUDGEMENT TESTS

QUESTION 37

> You are in charge of a team. You notice that one of the employees is continuously late. You have pulled him aside before to address the situation and he assured it would not happen again, but he continues to turn up late by approximately 20 minutes each time. What would you do?

A. Give him another chance and warn him if his lateness continues, further action will be taken.

B. Discuss his working hours, and try to find a way of allowing him to start later and finish later.

C. Issue a formal warning advising that he should improve his time keeping skills or further action will be taken.

D. Inform your colleague that you have no option but to dismiss him.

ANSWER OPTIONS

Very helpful	
Helpful	
Neither helpful nor unhelpful	
Unhelpful	
Very unhelpful	

QUESTION 38

> You are in a situation where first aid is required. Everyone at the company has had basic first aid training, and a colleague of yours has had a seizure. Nobody wants to help because they are unsure of the correct procedures. What would you do?

A. Put your colleague in the recovery position and wait for help.

B. Ask one of your colleagues to help whilst you phone for an ambulance.

C. Remain calm, get someone to call for an ambulance, and reassure your colleague whilst holding their head so they don't cause more injury.

D. Wait until your colleague's seizure has stopped, and ask them if they require an ambulance.

ANSWER OPTIONS

Very helpful	
Helpful	
Neither helpful nor unhelpful	
Unhelpful	
Very unhelpful	

QUESTION 39

> You work on the 30th floor of a block of offices. To get to and from your office, you always use the lift. You are at work when the fire alarm goes off. Company policy states that in an event of a fire, the lift is out of service. As you get up to leave the office, you notice that one of your colleagues has got in the lift. He knows you have seen him, and he is waving you in. What would you do?

A. Shout to get your colleague's attention and demand that he gets out of the lift.

B. Ignore what you have seen and continue walking down the stairs.

C. Walking down the stairs is a long way, so you decide to get in the lift with your colleague.

D. Abide by the company's rules and regulations and inform your colleague of that, before making your way down the stairs.

ANSWER OPTIONS

Very helpful	
Helpful	
Neither helpful nor unhelpful	
Unhelpful	
Very unhelpful	

QUESTION 40

> You are conducting an induction for three new employees, all of which will be working in the same department as you. You learn that one of the new employees has a heart condition called HCM (hypertrophic cardiomyopathy). She claims that she may experience shortness of breath, exercise intolerance and chest pains – all symptoms of her cardiac disease.

A. Tell her that you are fully committed to equal opportunities and she will not be treated any different to other members of staff.

B. Explain to her had you known this before employing her you would not have given her the job because you need someone whose work isn't going to be affected.

C. Ask her if there are any requirements she needs in order to make her more comfortable and anything she needs to accommodate her health.

D. Inform her that she may struggle with performing this job to a high standard, and therefore may want to reconsider accepting the job position.

ANSWER OPTIONS

Very helpful	
Helpful	
Neither helpful nor unhelpful	
Unhelpful	
Very unhelpful	

Now that you have completed this test, please check your answers carefully before moving onto the next section of the guide.

SUGGESTED ANSWERS TEST 2

SUGGESTED ANSWERS TEST 2

QUESTION 1

Very helpful – B

Helpful – C

Neither helpful nor unhelpful –

Unhelpful – D

Very unhelpful – A

Explanation:

B. Say yes. This is not a problem for you and you can see why moving desks would help her out and improve her working day.

This is **very helpful**. Not only does it improve her working environment, it also serves to improve/enhance relations within the office environment.

C. Tell her to speak to your boss first, to see if he is in agreement with her request. If he doesn't have a problem with it, neither do you.

This is **helpful**, simply because you are informing your boss what the proposed plan is regarding swapping desks.

D. Tell her you would be willing to swap desks providing she is prepared to move all of your belongings to the new desk.

This is **unhelpful**. Although you have agreed to the desk swap, the lady is in a wheelchair and may not be capable of moving all of your office belongings.

A. Say no. You are already settled in at your desk and to move would cause unnecessary upheaval.

This is **very unhelpful**. The lady is disabled and by not agreeing to her request you are failing to help improve her working environment. By choosing this option you will also serve to deteriorate your working relationship with both her and the rest of your team.

QUESTION 2

Very helpful –

Helpful – B

Neither helpful nor unhelpful – D

Unhelpful – A

Very unhelpful – C

Explanation:

B. Allow him to pay the full ticket fare to his intended stop.

This is **helpful** in the sense that you are showing compassion and common sense. However, technically the man is breaking the law by travelling without buying a ticket first. It could be argued that you should fine him. If everyone made this excuse and bought their tickets on the train instead, train operating companies could lose hundreds of thousands of pounds. There is also no way to ascertain whether he is lying about what stop he boarded at.

D. Kick him off at the next stop. The rules state that if he hasn't paid, then he must leave the train.

This is **neither helpful nor unhelpful**. Although he has broken the law, the man is not causing a disturbance on the train and has the money to pay the full fare.

A. Consult with the other people in the carriage as to what to do.

This is **unhelpful** and unprofessional. It's nothing to do with the other people in the carriage, and they shouldn't have to tell you how to do your job.

C. Perform a citizen's arrest. This man is a criminal.

This is **very unhelpful**. The man has done nothing to warrant a citizen's arrest, and certainly does not appear to be dangerous or in need of restraint.

QUESTION 3

Very helpful – C

Helpful – A

Neither helpful nor unhelpful – B

Unhelpful –

Very Unhelpful – D

Explanation:

C. Encourage your female colleagues to speak to your manager.

This is **very helpful** as it is the right thing to do. Although you should of course take some responsibility for helping your colleagues, ultimately it is their issue to take to the manager.

A. Take the new employee to one side and tell him that his behaviour needs to change.

This is **helpful**. You are taking steps to try and amend the situation, without going to management straight away. By discussing it with the new employee to one side, you are not humiliating them in front of your other colleagues.

B. Go to your manager and explain the situation.

This is **neither helpful nor unhelpful** as the woman has already said that she does not want to jeopardise the employee's position at the company. Therefore it is not up to you to go to management.

D. Ignore the behaviour. He's only joking.

This is **very unhelpful**. Sexual harassment/inappropriateness is a serious issue.

QUESTION 4

Very helpful – A

Helpful –

Neither helpful nor unhelpful – C

Unhelpful – B

Very unhelpful – D

Explanation:

A. Agree to act as a witness, but tell the chairman that there is no evidence to suggest sexism.

This is **very helpful**, as it is an honest response. If you have not seen any evidence of sexism, then you cannot support these claims. All you need to do is tell the chairman what you saw.

C. Agree to act a witness. Tell the chairman that you believe your sales manager is out of his depth, and that you would be better suited for his job.

This is **neither helpful nor unhelpful**. Although you are giving your opinion on matters, you certainly have no place telling the chairman that you should replace your manager.

B. Tell the chairman that you believe your sales manager was acting in a sexist manner.

This is **unhelpful**. As the passage states, you have seen no evidence of sexism.

D. Encourage your colleague to sue the company. Sexism is unacceptable.

This is **very unhelpful**. Not only have you seen no evidence of sexism, but suing the company would be extreme.

QUESTION 5

Very helpful – C

Helpful – B

Neither helpful nor unhelpful –

Unhelpful – D

Very unhelpful – A

Explanation:

C. Refuse to go, and encourage your colleague to do the same. This would be unprofessional.

This is **very helpful**. It would be extremely unprofessional to abandon your post just to go and get an autograph. Furthermore, the person might not want to be harassed. The fact that you have encouraged your colleague to do the same shows that you are thinking in the best interests of the company.

B. Tell your colleague that you won't be going anywhere. What they do is up to them.

This is **helpful**. This demonstrates that you are following the rules and standards. You are not the keeper of your other colleague, so you cannot force them to stay.

D. Take mobile pictures of the celebrity and post it on Twitter.

This is **unhelpful**. It is extremely unprofessional and could constitute an invasion of privacy, along with the fact that you could damage the reputation of the company by doing so.

A. Agree to cross over and get an autograph. This could be your only chance to meet such a prestigious person.

This is **very unhelpful**. It would be extremely unprofessional to abandon your post just to go and get an autograph. Furthermore, the celebrity might not want to be harassed.

QUESTION 6

Very helpful – D

Helpful – C

Neither helpful nor unhelpful –

Unhelpful – A

Very unhelpful – B

Explanation:

D. Take the man into a private room where you can write up a report of the incident, which will then be passed on to the police.

This is **very helpful** as it means that you have taken initiative, acted in a responsible manner and then passed the matter over to the organisation best equipped to deal with it. Along with this, you have made the man feel reassured that the case is in good hands.

C. Report the incident to senior station management. Tell the man that your company will be in touch.

This is **helpful**. This demonstrates that you are taking reasonable action in order to resolve the issue. Whilst you have been quite vague in terms of getting in contact with them, it still shows that you are acting upon it by going to management.

A. Offer to take the man's contact details, so that he can be reimbursed for a portion of his fare.

This is **unhelpful**. The man does not need to be reimbursed for his fare, he just wants his bag back.

B. Tell the man there is nothing that can be done.

This is **very unhelpful**. You are being extremely unsympathetic and unprofessional, along with refusing to take any responsibility.

QUESTION 7

Very helpful –

Helpful – A

Neither helpful nor unhelpful – D

Unhelpful – C

Very unhelpful – B

Explanation:

A. Ignore the situation. It's none of your business.

This is **helpful**, and is the best response to the question. Customer personal matters are nothing to do with staff, provided they aren't breaking laws or rules.

D. Ask the man for some dating advice.

This is **neither helpful nor unhelpful**. It could come across as unprofessional.

C. Take the man to one side and quietly ask him to explain his behaviour.

This is **unhelpful**. You have no right to speak to the man about his behaviour, regardless of how you feel about it. It is none of your business.

B. Confront the man on the spot. Cheating is immoral.

This is **very unhelpful**. Regardless of how you feel about the man's behaviour, it's none of your business.

QUESTION 8

Very helpful – B

Helpful –

Neither helpful nor unhelpful – C

Unhelpful – D

Very unhelpful – A

Explanation:

B. 'Mistakes happen. Let's pull the team together and brainstorm some ideas as to how we can fix this.'

This is **very helpful** as it allows you to try and reach a positive solution to the situation, whilst gaining suggestions from a wide variety of people.

C. 'Maybe you should consider whether this is the right position for you.'

This is **neither helpful nor unhelpful**. There will be time to discuss this after the incident has been resolved. All this will do is damage the employee's confidence, making him less likely to successfully complete further tasks.

D. 'I'd like you to apologise personally to the course attendees. You should explain the situation, and whose fault it is.'

This is **unhelpful**. You are essentially humiliating the employee in front of everyone.

A. 'Pack your bags. You're sacked.'

This is **very unhelpful**. Sacking the employee on the spot won't solve anything, and would be unprofessional.

QUESTION 9

Very helpful –

Helpful – A

Neither helpful nor unhelpful – D

Unhelpful – C

Very unhelpful – B

Explanation:

A. 'Hi. I'm really sorry about the incident that occurred yesterday. We hope to see you back at work soon.'

This is **helpful** because it shows a willingness to take responsibility for the incident and a level of care for the employee. The reason that this is not listed as very helpful is because you have failed to make reassurances that the incident is being looked into.

D. 'Hi. Do you think you could ring around and find someone else to cover your hours whilst you are off sick?'

This is **neither helpful nor unhelpful**. It is not the employee's job to find someone else to cover her hours, especially when they are sick.

C. 'Hi. Do you think you could come in and work on crutches?'

This is **unhelpful**. The employee is obviously unable to continue working on crutches and therefore would not benefit them or the company.

B. 'Hi. Unfortunately, since you are part time, and can no longer work, we are going to have to terminate your contract.'

This is **very unhelpful**. It shows a lack of care and professionalism, and is completely unfair on the employee, particularly since it was the company's fault to begin with.

QUESTION 10

Very helpful – B

Helpful – D

Neither helpful nor unhelpful – C

Unhelpful –

Very unhelpful – A

Explanation:

B. Take your manager to one side and question her on whether the claims are true. Explain why you needed the time off.

This is **very helpful** as it constitutes the most reasonable response. It shows professionalism and integrity.

D. Ring your manager in your own time to try and discuss the situation further.

This is **helpful** as it shows that you are looking to try and resolve the situation in a positive manner.

C. Arrange a team meeting to try to get to the bottom of this.

This is **neither helpful nor unhelpful** as you are involving your colleagues in a situation between you and your manager. You should be aiming to stop them gossiping or getting involved, therefore conducting a meeting will only make the situation worse.

A. Spread bad rumours about your manager. Two can play that game.

This is **very unhelpful** as it is extremely unprofessional, and could only lead to more trouble. You should be the better person.

QUESTION 11

Very helpful – C

Helpful – D

Neither helpful nor unhelpful –

Unhelpful – B

Very unhelpful – A

Explanation:

C. Apologise unreservedly for the toy not being in stock. Tell her that you will order the toy immediately from your supplier and then deliver it to her home as soon as it arrives. She will not be charged for either the toy or the delivery due to the inconvenience and stress caused.

This is **very helpful** as you are ordering the toy for her and delivering it for free. This will avoid any ill-feeling on the customer's part and will go some way to making good the mistake made by the shop.

D. Apologise unreservedly for the toy not being in stock. Tell her that you will order the toy immediately from your supplier and then deliver it to her home as soon as it arrives. She will be charged for the toy, but not for the delivery, due to the inconvenience and stress caused.

This is **helpful** as you are ordering the toy for her and delivering it direct to her. Although she has to pay for the toy you have agreed to deliver it for free, to compensate for the wasted journey. This will hopefully avoid any ill-feeling on the customer's part and will go part-way to making good the mistake made by the shop.

B. Apologise to the customer and inform her that there is another toy shop 15 miles away in the next town. If she travels there, they might have the toy she wants in stock.

This is **unhelpful**. Although you are informing her that another shop may sell the toy, the distance is excessive and you have not taken any steps to rectify the mistake made by the shop.

A. Apologise to the customer and say you are sorry but there is nothing more you can do.

This is **very unhelpful**. Although you are apologising you are doing nothing to resolve the issue or rectify the mistake made by the shop.

QUESTION 12

Very helpful – B

Helpful – C

Neither helpful nor unhelpful –

Unhelpful – A

Very unhelpful – D

Explanation:

B. Thank them for the money, but explain that you are unable to accept tips or financial rewards of this nature. Tell them that if they would like to give a reward, the supermarket supports local charities and they will be able to donate via their website.

This is **very helpful** as you are politely refusing the generous offer whilst not placing yourself in danger of being in breach of the company's strict policies regarding tips and financial rewards. Yet you are still giving the customer the option to donate to the supermarkets chosen charity.

C. Thank them for their kind offer, but explain that you are unable to accept tips or financial rewards of this nature.

This is **helpful** as you are politely refusing the generous offer whilst not placing yourself in danger of being in breach of the company's strict policies, regarding tips and financial rewards.

A. Thank them for the money, put it in your pocket, and leave a happy person. Nobody will ever know that you took the money, so there's no harm in taking it.

This is **unhelpful**. You are in breach of the company's strict policies regarding tips and financial rewards and you could be dismissed or disciplined if found out.

D. Walk away and ignore them.

This is **very unhelpful**. Whilst you are not placing yourself in danger of being in breach of the company's strict policies regarding tips and financial rewards, the way in which you are handling the situation is rude and will leave the customer feeling devalued and upset.

QUESTION 13

Very helpful – C

Helpful – B

Neither helpful nor unhelpful – D

Unhelpful –

Very unhelpful – A

Explanation:

C. Inform the responsible person at the warehouse that the wedges need to be moved immediately. Then, once you return to the office you will report the matter to your local Fire Safety Officer so that he/she can carry out a thorough inspection of the premise.

This is **very helpful**. Not only are you asking the responsible person to remove the wedges straight away, which educates them and makes the premise safer, you are also informing the Fire Service so they can carry out a thorough inspection of the premise.

B. Remove the wedges yourself and then report the situation to the local Fire Safety Officer when you return to your office later that day. He/she can then carry out a formal inspection.

This is **helpful**. Not only are you making the premise safer by removing the wedges whilst you are there, making the premise safer in the process, but you are also informing the Fire Service so they can carry out a thorough inspection of the premise.

D. Remove the wedges holding the doors open yourself and say nothing more about it.

This is **neither helpful nor unhelpful**. Whilst you are making the premise safer by removing the wedges yourself, it is likely they will be put back soon after.

A. Ignore it. You are at the premise to talk to the staff about a specific subject and it would be inappropriate to say anything there and then.

This is **very unhelpful**. As a Health and Safety assessor you have a responsibility to take action.

QUESTION 14

Very helpful – D

Helpful – C

Neither helpful nor unhelpful – B

Unhelpful –

Very unhelpful – A

Explanation:

D. Accept and embrace the changes. Change is part of working life. You would also try and explain the benefit of the changes to those who are sceptical.

This is **very helpful**. Not only are you embracing and accepting the changes, but you are also going out of your way to explain the benefit to others, which in turn improves the efficiency of the organisation.

C. Accept the changes yourself. It doesn't matter what the others think. After all, they are entitled to their own opinion.

This is **helpful**. Whilst you are not going the extra mile to educate your work colleagues on the benefit of change, you are accepting of them.

B. Keep your head down. Whilst you don't agree with the changes you don't want to get into trouble for raising your concerns.

This is **neither helpful nor unhelpful**. You are 'sort of' accepting the changes, despite disagreeing with them. In order for changes to be successful in any organisation, everyone must believe in them.

A. Join in with the objections. Why change things when everything is going OK as it is?

This is **very unhelpful**. Not only are you objecting to the change because everyone else is, you are also not being open to the opportunities that can be brought to the organisation. For an organisation to grow and develop, change is inevitable.

QUESTION 15

Very helpful – A

Helpful –

Neither helpful nor unhelpful – C

Unhelpful – B

Very unhelpful – D

Explanation:

A. Carry out the task as requested professionally, even though it will mean that you have to stay behind at work for an additional 10 minutes.

This is **very helpful** as you are willing to stay behind and do the job to the standard required, something which will be appreciated by your line manager.

C. Carry out the task to a slightly lesser standard, therefore finishing your shift on time.

This is **neither helpful nor unhelpful**. Although you are agreeing to do the task, you are not carrying it out to the required standard.

B. Inform your manager that you are going off duty in 5 minutes' time and that you won't be able to do the task to the required standard. Ask her if there is anyone else who can do the task.

This is **unhelpful** as the job will not get done if there is nobody else available.

D. Politely refuse to carry out the task.

This is **very unhelpful** as the task will not get done and the workplace will be left untidy for the oncoming shift.

QUESTION 16

Very helpful – B

Helpful – D

Neither helpful nor unhelpful –

Unhelpful – C

Very unhelpful – A

Explanation:

B. Hold a team meeting as soon as possible to establish the reasons why so many mistakes are being made. Then, formulate and agree a plan with all of the team in order to improve performance.

This is **very helpful** as you are communicating with the team to establish why the mistakes are being made. This will enable you to create a plan to improve performance that everyone can follow.

D. Speak to your boss and explain to her that you need to take on another member of staff to ease the pressure on the team.

This is **helpful**. If the mistakes are being made due to increased workload, it seems logical to employ another member of staff during this busy annual peak.

C. Get stuck in yourself more to help the team out. Clearly they are very busy and they could do with an extra pair of hands.

This is **unhelpful** because the team will see that you are failing to tackle the reasons why mistakes are being made. As their manager you are responsible for managing them, not doing their job for them.

A. Get the team together and tell them that, if matters do not improve, you will speak to the main boss about getting them replaced.

This is **very unhelpful**. Not only could this have a negative impact on team morale, you are also failing to establish why the mistakes are being made in the first place. If you dismiss the team and replace them with new staff, the same mistakes might not go away.

QUESTION 17

Very helpful – B

Helpful –

Neither helpful nor unhelpful - D

Unhelpful – C

Very unhelpful – A

Explanation:

B. Inform your manager that you are going to put the contents back on the shelf and request that you take your 10-minute tea break after the job is complete.

This is **very helpful**. Not only are you taking immediate action by putting the contents back on the shelf, but you are also ensuring that you get your tea break.

D. Forget about your tea break and put the contents back on the shelf yourself.

This is **neither helpful nor unhelpful**. The reason this is neither helpful nor unhelpful because you are being helpful because you are putting the contents back on the shelf, but overall it will not help your concentration and ability to perform well if you do not take your tea breaks.

C. Inform your manager that the contents have fallen on the floor and ask him if he can find someone else to put the contents back on the shelf as you are about to go on your tea break.

This is **unhelpful.** This is unhelpful because you are ultimately passing off the job to somebody else. You are not handling the situation yourself, and are hoping that someone else will tidy up while you go and have your tea break. This doesn't help the situation considering the store is already busy, and your other colleagues are probably already busy doing other duties.

A. Walk around the contents and go for your tea break. You are legally entitled to a break and someone else will be able to clear up the mess.

This is **very unhelpful**. Whilst you are entitled to your tea break, you are doing nothing about the issue. At the very least you should inform your manager so that someone else can start tidying up the mess.

QUESTION 18

Very helpful – B

Helpful – C

Neither helpful nor unhelpful - D

Unhelpful –

Very unhelpful – A

Explanation:

B. Apologise to the people in the queue and inform them that you will only be able to serve soft drinks and tea due to the breakdown of the coffee machine. Then, create a sign that says 'COFFEE MACHINE BROKEN – WE ARE ONLY ABLE TO SERVE SOFT DRINKS AND TEA – APOLOGIES FOR ANY INCONVENIENCE CAUSED' and place it on the shop door front so that people can make a decision whether or not they want to come in.

This is **very helpful**. Not only are you apologising to the customers, you are also offering people an alternative drink and you are also informing people of the issue before they enter the shop. This will save you considerable time having to explain to everyone who comes into the shop of the issue.

C. Apologise to each person as they reach the front of the queue and explain to them that you are unable to serve coffee but that you can serve them soft drinks or tea.

This is **helpful**. Although you will need to repeat yourself each time someone comes into the shop you are keeping the shop open and offering alternative drinks.

D. Call your boss and ask her what she wants you to do.

This is **neither helpful nor unhelpful**. Yes, you are doing something about the problem, but you are not working on your own initiative.

A. Apologise to the people in the queue and inform them you will not be able to serve them due to the breakdown of the coffee machine, which is beyond your control. Then, close the shop and make your way home.

This is **very unhelpful**. Whilst you are apologising to the customers, you are not offering them an alternative drink. You are simply giving up and going home.

QUESTION 19

Very helpful – C

Helpful –

Neither helpful nor unhelpful - D

Unhelpful – B

Very unhelpful – A

Explanation:

C. Listen to his concerns and allow him to vent his frustrations. Once he has finished, explain to him that there is a robust and thorough selection process in place and that unfortunately, on this occasion, he was unsuccessful and that someone else was found more suitable for the role. Then, offer him constructive feedback on his performance during the interview.

This is **very helpful**. You are allowing him to get his frustrations off his chest and you are giving him a valid reason for why he was unsuccessful. You are then offering him feedback on his performance so that he can improve for any future interviews he might attend.

D. Invite him to sit down and make him a cup of tea. Whilst you are out of the office, call your boss and ask for advice on how to deal with the situation.

This is **neither helpful nor unhelpful**. Although you are seeking advice on what to do next from your manager, you are not taking the lead and using your initiative to deal with the situation, something which would be expected from a supervisor.

B. Tell him that, although he was not successful this time, you will consider him for any future jobs that come up at the company.

This is **unhelpful**. You are potentially leading him along and giving him false hope. He will, quite rightly, expect to be successful at any future interviews he attends. This option just places you in a difficult position.

SUGGESTED ANSWERS TEST 2

A. Tell him you are not obliged to go into reasons why he was not successful and ask him to leave.

This is **very unhelpful**. Whilst you are correct in the fact that you are not obliged to go into the reasons why he was unsuccessful, this does not present your company in a positive light. It would just serve to make the situation worse.

QUESTION 20

Very helpful – A

Helpful – D

Neither helpful nor unhelpful -

Unhelpful – C

Very unhelpful – B

Explanation:

A. Apologise for the inconvenience that has been caused through the defective shaver. Explain to the customer the companies refund policy and that a receipt is required for a refund or exchange. However, explain to him that, if he can provide proof of purchase, by way of a card statement, that you will ask your manager if you can exchange the shaver for him.

This is **very helpful**. Although a receipt is required for exchange or refund, you are using your initiative and trying to find an alternative solution to rectify the problem.

D. Ask your manager what he thinks you should do.

This is **helpful**. Due to your position as a retail assistant it is good practice to ask your manager for advice.

C. Apologise for the inconvenience that has been caused through the defective shaver and then happily exchange the defective shaver for a new one.

This is **unhelpful**. You cannot exchange the shaver until you have proof it has been purchased from your store.

B. Explain to him that, because he does not have a receipt, you are not able to help him.

This is **very unhelpful**. Although you are correct in the fact that he needs a receipt in order to exchange the defective shaver, you are doing nothing at all to solve the problem.

QUESTION 21

Very helpful – A

Helpful – D

Neither helpful nor unhelpful - B

Unhelpful –

Very unhelpful – C

Explanation:

A. As soon as there becomes a natural break in her talk, raise your hand and explain that you are finding it difficult to understand most of what she is saying. Respectfully ask if she would please slow down so that you can take in all of the important information she is relaying.

This is **very helpful** as it is important that you understand what is being said at the meeting. If you wait until the end, your manager will have to go through the entire meeting again.

D. Wait until the end of the meeting and then ask your work colleagues for clarification on what she was saying.

This is **helpful** as you are seeking help from your other colleagues.

B. Wait to the end of the meeting before speaking to her in private and explain to her that you didn't understand most of what she was saying.

This is **neither helpful nor unhelpful**. Yes, you will get to hear everything that was said at the meeting; however, your manager will have to repeat all of the meeting points again, which will take considerable time.

C. Do nothing.

This is **very unhelpful** as you will never get to understand what was said during the meeting.

QUESTION 22

Very helpful – C

Helpful – A

Neither helpful nor unhelpful - B

Unhelpful – D

Very unhelpful –

Explanation:

C. Thank her for the information but explain that you do not want to pre-judge people and you want to have an entirely open mind. You will take him as you find him.

This is **very helpful** as you are not prepared to pre-judge people. After all, she may have a personal grudge against the manager and be deliberately trying to cause him harm.

A. Challenge her in a respectable manner and say that you think she is wrong for saying these things about a senior member of the team.

This is **helpful** as you are standing your ground and being firm about how you feel other members of the organisation are treated.

B. Thank her for the information and be on your guard from now on when dealing with your manager.

This is **neither helpful nor unhelpful**. Whilst it may appear to be a good thing to take on-board her comments, it is not a good thing to pre-judge people based on the comments or viewpoints of just one person.

D. Thank her for the information and then ask other people within the organisation if they have had the same experience whilst working with your manager.

This is **unhelpful**. You could end up discussing what you have heard with a member of the team who is close/supportive of the manager, and the gossip could get back to him, which might not be good for your future prospects.

QUESTION 23

Very helpful – D

Helpful – C

Neither helpful nor unhelpful - B

Unhelpful –

Very unhelpful – A

Explanation:

D. Agree to go to the hotel for the rest of the day and take your paperwork with you to do, whilst you are there.

This is **very helpful** as you are agreeing to go to the hotel and you will work on your paperwork whilst you are there.

C. Tell head office that you have lots of paperwork to catch up on but that you are prepared to ring around the other hotels in the region to see if there is another manager available to go to the hotel. If not, then you would be prepared to go and you would have to catch up with your paperwork another time.

This is **helpful** as you are offering to ring around to find another manager to cover. Failing that, you are prepared to go.

B. Explain to head office that you have lots of paperwork to catch up on and ask them how they want you to prioritise your work.

This is **neither helpful nor unhelpful**. You are a manager and you should be able to work out how to prioritise your own workload. Clearly, this shows a lack of professionalism and initiative.

A. Explain that you cannot meet their request as you have lots of paperwork to catch up on.

This is **very unhelpful** as it does nothing to help out head office.

QUESTION 24

Very helpful – A

Helpful – B

Neither helpful nor unhelpful - D

Unhelpful –

Very unhelpful – C

Explanation:

A. Speak to your colleague in private and ask him whether anything is wrong. You would also offer your support to see if you can help him through this difficult period he is going through.

This is **very helpful** as you are asking your colleague if there is anything wrong. Your colleague is likely to feel supported. This would be the best way to handle this type of situation.

B. Approach your manager in confidence and tell him that you think there might be something wrong with your work colleague, which is ultimately having an impact on hIs work performance.

This is **helpful** as you are raising your concerns with your manager and making him aware that there may be something more going on than first meets the eye. However, it is not very helpful, as it's not really your place to get involved.

D. Speak to your work colleague and offer to do some of his work for him in order to ease the pressure he is under from his manager.

This is **neither helpful nor unhelpful** as it does nothing to resolve the poor performance your colleague has been reprimanded for.

C. Do nothing. You do not want to interfere as it is not your problem.

This is **very unhelpful**. You are aware there is an issue, yet you are choosing to do nothing about it.

QUESTION 25

Very helpful – B

Helpful –

Neither helpful nor unhelpful - C

Unhelpful – A

Very unhelpful – D

Explanation:

B. Call your girlfriend and tell her you will be late coming home. Then, supervise the oncoming shift workers until their supervisor arrives.

This is **very helpful** and what would be expected of a supervisor in this type of role.

C. Call your boss and ask her what she thinks you should do.

This is **neither helpful nor unhelpful**. Your boss is likely to ask if you will wait for the oncoming supervisor to arrive anyway, so you may as well stay on and wait for him.

A. Tell the oncoming shift workers that they will have to work on their own, unsupervised, for 30 minutes until their supervisor arrives.

This is **unhelpful**. Whilst you are entitled to leave at the end of your shift, teamwork is important and you should be prepared to wait for the oncoming shift supervisor.

D. Just leave at the end of your shift. The fact that he is going to be late is not your problem.

This is **very unhelpful** as you are not even informing the oncoming shift workers that their supervisor will be late in.

QUESTION 26

Very helpful – D

Helpful –

Neither helpful nor unhelpful - B

Unhelpful – A

Very unhelpful – C

Explanation:

D. Arrange a meeting with your line manager to explain how you now feel ready to work more on your own, unsupervised. You would ask his permission for the supervision period to come to an end.

This is **very helpful** as you are discussing how you feel with the one person who really matters; your line manager. He can then make the decision whether or not to reduce the time period that you are supervised.

B. Tell your work colleagues how you feel and get their advice on what they think you should do.

This is **neither helpful nor unhelpful**. Whilst there is nothing wrong with speaking to your work colleagues, they are not the ones in the position to make a change to your supervised working.

A. Complete the 6-month supervision period as planned and not say anything about how you feel.

This is **unhelpful** as it is important to speak to your manager about your frustrations.

C. Start working more on your own without telling anyone.

This is **very unhelpful**. Your line manager would be extremely disappointed if you started working unsupervised, against his instructions. This could also lead to disciplinary procedures against you.

QUESTION 27

Very helpful – A

Helpful – D

Neither helpful nor unhelpful - B

Unhelpful –

Very unhelpful – C

Explanation:

A. Spend time with the team member to identify ways in which she can manage her time efficiently so that she can attend the team development meeting.

This is **very helpful** as you are showing support to the team member and you are also identifying ways to manage her time.

D. Get a member of staff from another team to cover the team member's workload during the day of the meeting so that she can attend.

This is **helpful** as it allows the team member to attend the team development meeting whilst her work is getting done.

B. Tell the team member that the team development meeting is mandatory. She must attend.

This is **neither helpful nor unhelpful** as it will only add stress to how she is feeling. It is not the most professional way to handle the situation.

C. Tell the team member that you understand how she is feeling and that she does not need to attend the team development meeting.

This is **very unhelpful** as you are failing to tackle the reasons why she is unable to cope with the increased workload. She is then more likely not to attend future meetings if she feels you give her permission not to attend. This also demonstrates to the other team members that it is OK to skip team meetings.

QUESTION 28

Very helpful – A

Helpful – B

Neither helpful nor unhelpful -

Unhelpful – C

Very unhelpful – D

Explanation:

A. You tell your colleague that he is being extremely unprofessional and tell him to arrange a lift home and sober up.

This is **very helpful**. It is important that everyone remains safe, and therefore an employee who is drunk could cause hazards. The employee needs to sober up before he can resume working.

B. You inform your colleague that you are aware of the said issue, and that he should seek help.

This is **helpful**. Whilst it would be a good suggestion for the man to seek help, at this moment in time, this is not going to help the current situation.

C. You get another one of your colleagues to drive him home, so you can continue working in peace.

This is **unhelpful**. Getting another colleague to drive him home is causing further disruption to the workplace, and therefore is causing more disorder.

D. You tell him to make a cup of coffee and sober up, and get on with his work quietly.

This would be **very unhelpful** because an employee who is drunk is not going to perform their duties to the best of their abilities, and therefore this will compromise their work.

QUESTION 29

Very helpful – D

Helpful – C

Neither helpful nor unhelpful - A

Unhelpful – B

Very unhelpful –

Explanation:

D. Sit them both down to try and resolve the issue, before continuing on with the project.

This is **very helpful**. Sitting both team members down and discussing how to resolve the situation not only shows professionalism, but it also handles the situation in a mature and efficient manner.

C. Sit the individual in question down, and ask their side of the story.

This option is **helpful**. Sitting the individual in question down, and asking their side of the story shows that you are working towards resolving the issue by gaining a full understanding of what is happening.

A. Explain to your team member that the group need her, and that she should rise above it and continue with the project.

This is **neither helpful nor unhelpful**. Even though this will boost your team member's confidence, again this does not deal with the current situation.

B. Wait to see if you hear anything as mentioned by the individual, and then take action.

This is **unhelpful**. Waiting to see if anything happens is not dealing with the current situation. It shows that you do not believe your team member, and shows a lack of initiative at handling difficult situations.

QUESTION 30

Very helpful – D

Helpful –

Neither helpful nor unhelpful - B

Unhelpful – A

Very unhelpful – C

Explanation:

D. Ask your colleagues to help you with the additional information, so that you can ensure the work gets added.

This is a **very helpful** response. Asking for help from your colleagues will allow you to get the extra information added in time for the presentation. It shows that you are willing to take help from other people, and will therefore be able to complete the presentation to a better standard.

B. Inform your boss that whilst you cannot add in this information due to time constraints, you will be happy to answer any questions they have.

This is **neither helpful nor unhelpful**. While inviting people in to ask questions at the end of the presentation, this will not demonstrate all of the important information that has been missed in the presentation. This doesn't fix your presentation, and will suggest that you run out of time to complete the presentation.

A. Explain to your boss that the presentation is being presented that afternoon, and you do not have enough time to add in that information.

This is **unhelpful**. Not adding in the information to the presentation means that you're going to go into the presentation knowing that important information has been left off.

C. Ignore your boss' concerns and present the presentation the way it is.

This option is **very unhelpful**. Ignoring your boss' comments regarding the presentation does not fix the issues, nor does it deal with the situation.

QUESTION 31

Very helpful – C

Helpful –

Neither helpful nor unhelpful - D

Unhelpful – A

Very unhelpful – B

Explanation:

C. Negotiate your time off with your boss and reiterate that you are allowed said number of days off.

Option C is **very helpful**. By negotiating your time off with your boss shows that you are being considerate, and willing to negotiate your days off in terms of convenience.

D. Discuss with your boss the importance of employment contracts, which reiterate the number of vacation days an employee is allowed.

Option D is **neither helpful nor unhelpful**. This would not improve or make the situation worse.

A. Take the vacation days as advised by the Human Resources department.

Option A is **unhelpful** because you want to ensure that your holiday does not conflict with any of your workload. This should be discussed with your boss.

B. Decide not to take your vacation days if it is going to upset the boss.

Option B is **very unhelpful**. The Human Resources department have advised that you take your days off during this slow period and not taking them off, might mean you won't be able to take them if your workload increases.

QUESTION 32

Very helpful – C

Helpful – A

Neither helpful nor unhelpful - B

Unhelpful –

Very unhelpful – D

Explanation:

C. Bring up this issue in a polite conversation with your Managing Director, and voice what your colleagues are feeling.

Option C is **very helpful**. Bringing the issue up to your Managing Director is the best way to handle the situation. Your Managing Director is your friend, and therefore he is more likely to listen to what you have to say. Informing him of what is going on will give him time to resolve the issue.

A. Try to talk to your colleagues about the situation and show that you understand how they must be feeling.

Option A is **helpful**. Talking to your colleagues and showing empathy and consideration will allow your colleagues to open up more to you, so you can help the situation.

B. Continue being good friends with the Managing Director and not say anything to him. He is a clever man, and will soon realise that his behaviour is unacceptable.

This is **neither helpful nor unhelpful**. Saying nothing to the Managing Director does not deal with the situation, that is likely to escalate if the issue is not resolved.

D. Ignore what your colleagues are saying. You are in the good books, and you don't want to stir anything up that may jeopardise your position.

This option is **very unhelpful**. Ignoring what your colleagues are saying is likely to cause a tense working atmosphere. Ignoring something does not resolve the issue, nor will it go away.

SUGGESTED ANSWERS TEST 2

QUESTION 33

Very helpful – A

Helpful – B

Neither helpful nor unhelpful -

Unhelpful – D

Very unhelpful – C

Explanation:

A. Send a follow-up email immediately after apologising for the mistake. Send the email to the correct person.

Option A is **very helpful**. Sending a follow-up email immediately apologising for your mistake, shows a strong reaction to handling difficult situations efficiently and professionally. You need to fix any errors that you cause.

B. Send the email again, but this time to the correct person. The person you sent the email to will just assume it's a mistake.

This is **helpful**. Sending the email again to the correct person means that the important client information has been sent to the correct person. However, it is not very helpful because you have disregarded the fact that you have also sent it to someone else.

D. Explain the situation to your manager, and let him deal with resolving the issue.

This is **unhelpful**. Explaining the issue to the manager and letting him deal with your mistake shows a lack of professionalism. You are passing the error to somebody else, instead of making amends.

C. Leave the office, and deal with the issue first thing in the morning.

This is **very unhelpful**. Leaving the office and dealing with the issue in the morning does not deal with the situation immediately. Some situations require an immediate action, and this issue is one of them.

QUESTION 34

Very helpful – D

Helpful – C

Neither helpful nor unhelpful - B

Unhelpful – A

Very unhelpful –

Explanation:

D. Bring it up in discussion at the next team meeting and ensure everyone understands how powerful topics such as religion or politics are discouraged at the working environment.

This is **very helpful**. Bringing this topic up in discussion at the next team meeting will not only get straight to the point, but it also addresses the team as a whole, and not just singling someone out. This is the best way to ensure that topics like this are kept to a minimum.

C. Comfort your colleague who has been upset by the discussion, and tell her to speak to the new colleague about this upset.

Option C is **helpful**. Comforting your colleague who was upset by the discussion, and telling her to speak to the new colleague will allow the situation to be addressed quickly. The new colleague needs to see that his discussions are affecting other people.

B. Inform your new colleague how important first impressions are.

This is **neither helpful nor unhelpful**. Talking about first impressions after they've already happened will not serve to remedy the situation.

A. Voice your opinions regarding religion and demonstrate that everyone is different.

Option A is **unhelpful**. Voicing your own opinions on religion could possibly make the situation worse. Topics such as religion should not be discussed at the workplace because they are extremely personal, and therefore joining in the conversation with your own views doesn't show that you handle difficult situations in the best way.

QUESTION 35

Very helpful – A

Helpful –

Neither helpful nor unhelpful - B

Unhelpful – C

Very unhelpful – D

Explanation:

A. Discuss with your ex about the situation, and come to some agreement so that you can both continue to work in a comfortable environment.

This is **very helpful**. Trying to come to some common ground between you and your ex will allow you to both work in a comfortable working environment. Personal matters should not jeopardise the integrity of the job role – you must remain professional.

B. Ask your colleagues what their problem is – it's none of their business what has happened between you and your ex.

This is **neither helpful nor unhelpful**. Asking your colleagues what their problem is, is not going to help matters.

C. Inform the Head of the Department that you are unable to work in such a hostile environment, and want to be relocated to a different department.

Option C is **unhelpful**. Informing the Head of Department that you wish to be transferred to a different department just because of an ex is unprofessional. You should be able to find a way to maintain a healthy working environment, and not let personal matters get in the way of performing your job role.

D. Avoid the colleagues that are making it difficult for you, and continue on with your daily routine.

This is **very unhelpful**. Avoiding colleagues that are making it difficult for you is immature and unprofessional. This is guaranteed to disrupt productivity by not working as a team.

QUESTION 36

Very helpful –

Helpful – C

Neither helpful nor unhelpful - A

Unhelpful – B

Very unhelpful – D

Explanation:

C. Confront your colleague and inform her about company policy in regards to taking company property.

This option is **helpful**. Confronting your colleague and reminding her of company policy is a great way to make a subtle point, but not directly accusing her.

A. Do nothing. You do not have enough evidence to go by, and if she is guilty, she will be found out soon.

This is **neither helpful nor unhelpful**. Ignoring the situation and pretending not to know anything does not deal with the situation, and shows a lack of initiative.

B. Decide that you don't have enough evidence yet, so you will need to gather more evidence to catch her out.

This option is **unhelpful**. Deciding to gather up more information yourself is taking matters in to your own hands, which is not your responsibility.

D. Inform your manager that your colleague is responsible for the large amounts of company property going missing.

This is **very unhelpful**. Informing your manager that your colleague is responsible for the large amounts of company property going missing is misleading, considering you haven't witnessed large amounts of property being stolen by her. You only witnessed her putting stationery in her bag, which might have been hers; therefore, you could not jump to such a hasty conclusion.

SUGGESTED ANSWERS TEST 2

QUESTION 37

Very helpful – B

Helpful – C

Neither helpful nor unhelpful - A

Unhelpful –

Very unhelpful – D

Explanation:

B. Discuss his working hours, and try to find a way of allowing him to start later and finish later.

Option B is **very helpful**. Discussing working hours and working out whether the employee would like to start later and finish later is in everyone's best interests, and will hopefully fix the issue of lateness.

C. Issue a formal warning advising that he should improve his time keeping skills or further action will be taken.

Option C is **helpful**. Issuing a formal warning after the employee has been warned previously shows that you are taking stronger action regarding the situation.

A. Give him another chance and warn him if his lateness continues, further action will be taken.

This option is **neither helpful nor unhelpful**. Giving him another chance even though you have given him chances before is unlikely to make the situation better. You need to take stricter action for their continuous lateness.

D. Inform your colleague that you have no option but to dismiss him.

This is **very unhelpful**. Informing your colleague that you have no option but to dismiss him does not handle the situation in the best way. You need to understand why the employee has been turning up late, and find out whether there are ways to rectify this.

QUESTION 38

Very helpful – C

Helpful – B

Neither helpful nor unhelpful -

Unhelpful – A

Very unhelpful – D

Explanation:

C. Remain calm, get someone to call for an ambulance, and reassure your colleague whilst holding their head so they don't cause more injury.

Option C is **very helpful**. Getting someone to call an ambulance, and holding the person's head still so they don't cause more injury demonstrates great first aid. This should be done until the ambulance arrives, so they can begin their treatment.

B. Ask one of your colleagues to help whilst you phone for an ambulance.

This is **helpful**. Asking for extra help from other colleagues will allow you to call for an ambulance, and ensure that your colleague is still being looked after.

A. Put your colleague in the recovery position and wait for help.

Option A is **unhelpful**. If someone is having a seizure, it doesn't mean that they need to be put in the recovery position.

D. Wait until your colleague's seizure has stopped, and ask them if they require an ambulance.

Option D is **very unhelpful**. Waiting for your colleague to stop having their seizure to ask them if they require an ambulance, could potentially be life threatening. Immediate medical attention is required.

QUESTION 39

Very helpful – D

Helpful – A

Neither helpful nor unhelpful -

Unhelpful – B

Very unhelpful – C

Explanation:

D. Abide by the company's rules and regulations and inform your colleague of that, before making your way down the stairs.

Option D is **very helpful**. Abiding by the company rules and regulations and informing your colleague of these rules, demonstrates that you are following company policy. Continuing down the stairs shows that you too, are following company policy and you have reminded your colleague of expected behaviour.

A. Shout to get your colleague's attention and demand that he gets out of the lift.

Option A is **helpful** because it is warning your colleague to get out of the lift. Shouting is the only way to get their attention over the fire alarm continuing to sound.

B. Ignore what you have seen and continue walking down the stairs.

This is **unhelpful**. Ignoring what you have seen and continuing to walk down the stairs does not handle the situation, instead you are playing ignorant to a possibly hazardous situation.

C. Walking down the stairs is a long way, so you decide to get in the lift with your colleague.

This is **very unhelpful**. Getting in the lift as well, despite knowing that you are not allowed to use the lift during fire alarms is unprofessional, and possibly dangerous. This does not deal with the situation in the best possible way.

QUESTION 40

Very helpful – C

Helpful –

Neither helpful nor unhelpful - A

Unhelpful – D

Very unhelpful – B

Explanation:

C. Ask her if there are any requirements she needs in order to make her more comfortable and anything she needs to accommodate her health.

Option C is **very helpful**. Asking her if she needs any requirements to accommodate her shows that you take equal opportunities seriously, and are willing to make her feel comfortable in the workplace. This demonstrates great personal skills, and strong professionalism.

A. Tell her that you are fully committed to equal opportunities and she will not be treated any different to other members of staff.

This option is **neither helpful nor unhelpful**. Suggesting that she should not be treated any different, despite her medical conditions, shows a lack of empathy and discriminates against her condition. You need to ensure that the working environment is safe for the new employee, and support her in any way possible.

D. Inform her that she may struggle with performing this job to a high standard, and therefore may want to reconsider accepting the job position.

Option D is **unhelpful**. Telling her that she may want to reconsider the job position, suggests that you are trying to palm her off. Again, this is unacceptable and discriminatory behaviour.

B. Explain to her had you known this before employing her you would not have given her the job because you need someone whose work isn't going to be affected.

This option is **very unhelpful**. This is discriminatory behaviour which is unacceptable. Therefore, telling her that you would not have employed her had you known of her medical condition, is unprofessional.

TEST 3
(Non Train Driver related)

TEST 3 (NON TRAIN DRIVER RELATED)

In this third and final test, you are required to read a short description of a fictitious scenario, before choosing just one option from the four listed, based on what you would do next. Take a look at the following sample question.

SAMPLE QUESTION

You are a qualified labourer and it is your first day working on a new building site. You arrive at the site and start putting on your personal protective equipment (PPE). One of the senior labourers at the site comes up to you and tells you that, 'you don't need to wear that gear mate'. He continues to say, 'the site foreman here is really relaxed and he isn't that bothered whether you wear it or not'. What would you do?

A. Tell him thanks and put your PPE back in your bag. You don't want to wear the equipment if nobody else is wearing it as it will make you look silly.

B. Tell him thanks but that you will be wearing your PPE as you don't want to get injured if anything dangerous were to happen.

C. Tell him thanks but that you will be wearing your PPE and you suggest everyone else does, too. It's a legal requirement for everyone on the site to wear personal protective equipment.

D. Tell him thanks for the advice but that you will just wear your hardhat and nothing else. It's important to protect your head at the very least. This way, you won't look as silly amongst the other workers.

How to answer the question

As per the instructions, you are only required to choose one answer from the four presented options. It is important to answer each question honestly; however, you should also learn from each question that is presented and decide which is the most appropriate answer.

In the above sample question, the most appropriate answer is option C. There is a legal requirement for all workers on the site to wear PPE and you must

TEST 3 (Non Train Driver related)

have the confidence to be assertive in situations of this nature. You must also take responsibility for informing others of the legal requirement. In this case, this is the senior labourer who is speaking to you.

Although this type of question has nothing to do with the role of a Train Driver, it is assessing your ability to work safely whilst adhering to safe-working protocols in order to abide by company rules and regulations.

Now that you understand how to answer the questions, please attempt the following test. There are 20 questions and you have 20 minutes to complete them. The answers are provided at the end of the test.

QUESTION 1

> You are a Project Leader and manage four other team members. Two of the team members have told you they won't be able to meet the deadlines of the project. The director of the organisation reminds you about the importance of meeting deadlines. Which is the most likely course of action you would take?

A. Adapt the workload for all Team Members to respect the deadlines.

B. Discuss with the two Team Members that are having difficulties and identify the causes, evaluate the remaining workload before determining an action plan to finish the project.

C. Ask the two team members that won't submit their work in time, to work additional hours in order to respect the deadlines.

D. Inform your Director of the situation. Justify the status on the project, and ask for additional resources.

ANSWER

TEST 3 (Non Train Driver related)

QUESTION 2

> During your annual assessment with your Team Leader, he tells you that he thinks you could decrease your thinking time to make decisions quicker, in order to handle more tasks. The tasks that you are undertaking are complex in nature. Which of the following options would you be most likely to do?

A. Justify it with the fact that the guidelines are not always clear and that you are taking time to clarify them.

B. Justify it by saying that the complexity of the tasks require more thinking time.

C. Reduce your thinking time and spend less time dedicated to quality.

D. Keep your own way of working, but do overtime to handle more tasks.

ANSWER

QUESTION 3

> You are working in a supermarket and you have an annoying work colleague. He is a perfectionist and pays attention to every little detail. He seems to continuously pay attention to every detail, which in turn holds up the task, even when the workload is significant and the team is already having difficulties meeting deadlines. This behaviour really upsets and irritates you. Which of the following options would you be most likely to do?

A. Just get on with the task and pretend he isn't there.

B. Discuss how you feel with your line manager and mention the challenges your team are facing due to the working style of your work colleague.

C. Discuss how you feel with your work colleague and mention to him the challenges the team are facing due to his working style.

D. During the next team meeting, mention this issue and challenge your work colleague's working style in front of the rest of the group.

ANSWER

QUESTION 4

> You are a supervisor working in a warehouse which operates 24-hours a day. A member of your team asks you to permit him flexible working hours, as he prefers to work at night. You give your approval. However, after a couple of weeks you notice a decline in his productivity, which delays his tasks getting done. Which of the following options would you be most likely to do?

A. Talk with your team member and explain to him that this situation cannot continue. You decide to immediately cancel the flexible working agreement.

B. Ask another team member of your team to take over his tasks in order to improve productivity.

C. Decide to just accept the delayed projects.

D. Discuss the issue with the team member and ask whether there is anything affecting his performance. Then, explain to him that you expect to see an improvement in his performance and agree with him set targets.

ANSWER

QUESTION 5

> Due to the economic crisis, the budget of your organisation has been reduced. The head of your department announces that significant changes will occur, which in turn will affect everyone in the department. He also states that nobody will be made redundant. The action plan will be presented soon. Which of the following options would you be most likely to do?

A. Continue your work as normal and remain attentive to the announcements being made. Change within any organisation is to be expected.

B. Talk to your colleagues to get information. Some people are always informed early of the future changes.

C. Share your concerns with the head of department.

D. Ask to get a meeting with management to learn of the changes before the official meeting.

ANSWER

QUESTION 6

> You are working on a project with two colleagues from another team. Since the beginning, the working relations have been strained. You feel as though you are constantly being criticised and that the planning of the project has been decided without you. Which of the following options would you be most likely to do?

A. Ask to be replaced from the project.

B. Ask your Team Leader to attend the next meeting so he can see what is going on.

C. Discuss how you feel with your colleagues and indicate to them that you expect better collaboration for the remainder of the project.

D. Discuss how you feel with the colleague with whom you have the best relation; mention your perception and hope for a change.

ANSWER

QUESTION 7

> You are working in an office as an administrator. One of your work colleagues, who is married, has been cheating with other women within the team. Which of the following options would you be most likely to do?

A. Ignore the situation. It's none of your business.

B. Confront the man on the spot. Cheating is immoral.

C. Speak to your colleague in private and indicate your dissatisfaction at his behaviour. Also explain how you feel his behaviour could have an impact on the team and the effectiveness of the organisation.

D. Ask the man for some dating advice.

ANSWER

QUESTION 8

> You are on your way to work. Up ahead you notice a lot of traffic. You get stuck in traffic for 30 minutes. You are listening to the radio traffic updates and realise that you are stuck in traffic because of a car collision. There is no way of turning back or changing direction, so you have to sit and wait for the traffic to start moving. You are unsure about what time that will be. The issue is that you've already had 2 warnings about turning up to work late, and you are scared about the consequences if you arrive late.

A. Wait until you know what time you will arrive at work before phoning in late.

B. Phone your team leader and tell them about your current situation.

C. Keep your Managing Director regularly updated on your whereabouts and your expected time of arrival.

D. Text one of your colleagues and ask them to cover for you until you get to work.

ANSWER

QUESTION 9

> Leaving valuable property in the drawers of your desk is discouraged. Staff are notified on employment that the company cannot accept any responsibility for loss or damage of personal property if left unattended. You left your mobile in the drawer of your desk and it's now missing. Two weeks go by, and you notice that one of your colleagues has shown up to work with a phone identical to yours.

A. Go over to your colleague and immediately demand back the phone.

B. Go to management and inform them that one of your colleagues has stolen your phone.

C. Ask management to look at CCTV in order to establish if the colleague went into your desk and took the phone.

D. Ask your colleague to borrow the phone and then not give it back.

ANSWER

TEST 3 (Non Train Driver related)

QUESTION 10

> You are made the Operations Manager for the company. It is a position that you have been working towards for several months. However, you feel as though you are out of your comfort zone, and are unsure whether you are competent for the job role.

A. Speak with your Managing Director and inform him of your concerns and ask for advice.

B. Ask your colleagues what they would do in your situation.

C. Continue on working, and hope that you improve on the job.

D. Realise that you are not cut out for the position and hand in your resignation.

ANSWER

QUESTION 11

> You have been made Project Leader. You have established a plan and prepared the task allocation, which you present to your team. For one particular task, there are no volunteers. How do you decide to allocate the work?

A. Communicate the importance of the project to your team, encourage them, and reaffirm your request for a volunteer.

B. Based on the skills of your team members, you decide on the best allocation.

C. Assign the work to a team member that already undertook similar tasks in the past.

D. Assign the work to a team member who has the lowest workload.

ANSWER

QUESTION 12

> You have been working in a team for several years, and you wish to advance to a role with more responsibilities in a particular department. In order to get a promotion, you need to improve on certain skills that you have. Your plan is to get a promotion within a few months. What course of action do you take?

A. Do your best to demonstrate an excellent work-rate during that period in order to get the best evaluation possible, which could convince your Head of Unit to promote you.

B. Discuss your desires with the people already involved in that department to identify the skills required in order to get a promotion.

C. Discuss with your Head of Unit your desires to get promoted and request an assessment of your strengths and weaknesses. Then, request a training development plan to assist you in your promotional goals.

D. You know your weaknesses and decide to follow several training programmes in order to improve your skills.

ANSWER

QUESTION 13

> You are working on a team project. During a meeting to discuss the methodology of working, you present your plan. One of your colleagues interrupts you and challenges the validity of your plan. He offers up an alternative plan, which the rest of the group agrees with. You are an expert in this field and notice some inconsistencies in his plan. How do you react?

A. As you are an expert in this particular field, you challenge the plan of your colleague. You list all inconsistencies in his plan and highlight the benefits of yours.

B. Accept the plan of your colleague as the team has validated them. Then, following the meeting, meet with your project leader to express your concerns about his plan.

C. Accept the plan of your colleague as the team has validated it. Keep your plan saved to use it during the project if needed.

D. Tell your colleague that you find his plan interesting, but that you notice inconsistencies that could lead to issues later. Explain what the inconsistencies are and then suggest alternative ways to complete the project with an adapted plan that everyone agrees with.

ANSWER

QUESTION 14

A member of a department is working on analysis for her team leader. The team leader asks her to identify the correlations in some financial data so the department can work on the recommendations. Following the completion of the analysis, a meeting is scheduled at the end of the week to discuss the results so a plan can be put in place to make the necessary improvements. However, the member of the department who is working on the analysis feels that it is too early and requires an additional week to finalise her analysis. How should she proceed?

A. Prior to the meeting, present the analysis that she has identified so far and inform her team leader of the additional time required to finalise the task.

B. Ask the team leader to postpone the meeting in order to finalise the analysis she is working on.

C. Present her initial findings as they are, and not tell her team leader that they are incomplete.

D. Work additional hours in order to finalise her work before the meeting with her team leader.

ANSWER

QUESTION 15

> You are a team leader. A report presenting the activity of your team is showing a loss of productivity amongst the department. You have detected some procedures that haven't been correctly followed, leading to errors. How do you solve the issues?

A. Discuss the problem with other team leaders within the organisation to identify if such issues have occurred in the past, and what was put in place to solve them.

B. Ask your manager for a performance audit in order to get some support in resolving these issues.

C. Organise a team meeting for the whole department, explain your findings and look for ways to make improvements, collectively.

D. Organise a team meeting for the whole department and remind the workforce of the guidelines and the importance of individual contributions in order to reach the objectives.

ANSWER

TEST 3 (Non Train Driver related)

QUESTION 16

> An employee survey has revealed that within the organisation you work for, stress levels are high and motivation levels are low among staff. The head of unit asks you to monitor the productivity of your team and do all you can to avoid resignations, because this would have a negative impact on the productivity of the organisation. What would you do?

A. Monitor the performance and behaviour of your team members and assess those showing signs of stress in order to provide support.

B. In order to assess the performance of your team, and to get the bottom of the problems, you decide to organise individual meetings with each team member.

C. During a team meeting, ask your team members what could be done to improve the working environment and to reduce the stress levels.

D. To improve the working environment and increase motivation levels, you ask a team member to organise a regular team-building event outside of working hours.

ANSWER

QUESTION 17

> One of your work colleagues, Tim, is arrogant and thinks he is the strongest person within the team. The team makes comments about him behind his back. Tim confides in you and complains about the cold and unfriendly atmosphere he feels within the team. He is asking you for your opinion. What would you do?

A. Avoid the subject by saying you feel the atmosphere is good within the team.

B. For his own benefit, tell him in private what the other colleagues are thinking. This will help him to make changes to his attitude and his approach to the team, if he chooses to.

C. Tell him that everyone, including you, thinks he is arrogant and he has been doing nothing to improve the working relations with his team members.

D. Tell him that you think he needs to speak to the other members of the team to find out what the problem is.

ANSWER

QUESTION 18

> You have joined a new team. Even though you have several years' worth of previous experience, it is a new role for you. Your team leader is reviewing each file that you have been working on. He is making significant changes and recommendations to every file you have worked on. You feel extremely frustrated that so many changes are needed. How do you react?

A. Take on board and respect your team leader's changes and put more energy and focus into working on files in the future. By having a positive attitude, you hope that the number of changes in the future will decrease.

B. Discuss with your colleagues your feelings and see if your team leader has made significant changes to their work before, and if so, find out why he is doing this.

C. Ask your team leader for feedback to show that you are determined and to demonstrate your willingness to improve the quality of your work. By having a positive attitude and taking this approach to the situation, you hope that the number of changes in the future will decrease.

D. Ask a more experienced colleague to review your files first before submitting them to your team leader.

ANSWER

QUESTION 19

> You are working on a project as part of a team. The majority of your colleagues will finish their work on time. However, three of your colleagues are having difficulties getting their work done, and as a result, this is holding up the project. The three colleagues who are having difficulties have approached you and requested assistance in getting the job complete. The project leader is away on business travel, and he has asked you to supervise the work whilst he is away. He stated it is imperative that the work gets completed on time. What would you do?

A. Organise an informal team meeting and establish an action plan to finalise the project by providing support to the three work colleagues.

B. Report these problems to the project leader and ask him for advice on the best way to approach this situation. After all, you are not the official team leader and are only standing in for him whilst he is away.

C. Tell the three work colleagues who are having difficulties that they need to improve their performance, or they will let the rest of the team down. If everyone else within the team can finish their work on time, so can they.

D. Tell the three work colleagues that you will personally step in and help them to get the work completed on time. You do not want to let your team leader down, so you will do what it takes to get the project completed for his return.

ANSWER

QUESTION 20

> You are working as a security guard for a local firm. Your team leader comes in to a meeting with an aggressive attitude towards a colleague, who made a mistake when completing the security log at the end of the last shift. It is the first time that you have seen your team leader reacting this way. Your colleague tells you that he is demotivated and stressed out, and that he hadn't realised he had made the mistake. What would you do?

A. Discuss the impact that your leader's aggressive attitude is having on the team, with your head of unit.

B. Avoid making any judgement and do not get involved as it does not concern you.

C. Discuss it with your colleague and check whether or not he requires some support in his job to ensure he does not make the mistake again.

D. Speak to your team leader in private about how your colleague is feeling and tell her that you disagree with how she approached the situation in the meeting.

ANSWER

Now you have completed the final test, please check over your answers in the next section.

SUGGESTED ANSWERS TEST 3

SUGGESTED ANSWERS TEST 3

1. B

This is the most effective answer because it shows that you are taking full responsibility for the issue. You are discussing the problem with the employees, identifying the issues and putting a plan in place to get the project completed.

2. B

Option B is effective simply because you are explaining to your line manager that the task is complex in nature, and as such requires further thinking time in order to complete the high standards required. You are telling your boss the exact reason why there is a delay. He/she can then decide on what steps to take next, if appropriate.

3. C

The most effective, professional and mature way to deal with situations of this nature, is to speak to the person direct in a constructive manner.

4. D

In this situation you have already demonstrated a degree of flexibility to meet his demands. It is correct that you speak to him to find out if there is anything that might be affecting his performance before expecting an improvement which will be monitored through set targets.

5. A

It is only right that you remain attentive to any announcements and that you are understanding and open to the change that is coming. Change happens in all organisations and you need to embrace and accept it.

6. C

In this type of scenario, the only effective way to deal with it, is to speak directly to your work colleagues. This demonstrates confidence, resilience and an ability to assert your position and how you are feeling.

SUGGESTED ANSWERS TEST 3

7. C

Most people, in this type of situation, would choose answer option A. However, your work colleague's behaviour could, and most likely will, have an impact on the team at some point in the near or distant future. Therefore, it is only right that you speak to him in private and express your concerns. Whilst you cannot force him to change his behaviour, you can hopefully encourage him to think about how his actions could impact the people around him.

8. B

Phoning your team leader and informing them about your current situation is the best way to handle this situation. Although option C seems reasonable, you should go to your team leader before informing your managing director. Your team leader will be responsible for you and therefore this should be your first line of contact.

9. C

Response C is a helpful response, as you are not simply jumping to conclusions. Asking to see CCTV will allow you to see whether or not your colleague did steal your phone.

10. A

Response A is very helpful. Speaking to someone in a higher position and informing him of your concerns not only shows that you have taken initiative, but it quickly deals with the issue. By speaking to someone in a higher position, will guarantee to provide resolutions to improve the situation.

11. B

If no one volunteers for the task, it is your responsibility as project leader to designate assignments. This can be done by tailoring the task to the best suited person based on skill. Even if a person volunteered, you may not have the most ideal person completing the task. Therefore, it would be best to choose someone yourself, based on who you think would be most suited to complete it.

12. C

The best option here is to discuss your promotion aspirations with your manager. He/she will be fully aware of your strengths and weaknesses and will be able to assist you in your development, which in turn will help you achieve promotion.

13. D

Option D not only acknowledges your work colleagues plan, but it also explains why you feel there are inconsistencies. You are an expert after all, and you must explain your concerns. However, it is also good practice to seek alternative methods for working that the entire team agrees with.

14. D

This is the most effective option available as working additional hours will ensure that all of the information is included before finalising the work.

15. C

Clearly the most effective option here is to discuss the problems with your department in order to identify ways to solve the errors occurring. During the meeting the team may explain to you the reasons why the problems have been occurring. This will then empower you to make the changes necessary to improve performance.

16. B

By speaking to each member of the team individually, you will be able to identify any concerns each team member has. This will empower you to make the necessary changes required in order to reduce stress levels and increase motivation within the department.

17. B

By speaking to Tim in private, and by stating what you think the problem is, you are giving him the opportunity to make some changes to how he portrays himself to the rest of the team. It is then down to him whether or not he takes on-board your comments.

18. C

This option demonstrates a mature and professional approach to your role. This type of attitude will be appreciated by your team leader.

19. A

The most effective way to deal with this type of scenario is to hold a team meeting and put a plan of action in place to get the work completed.

20. C

This is a very difficult situation to deal with; however, the most effective approach is to offer support to your colleague and see if there is any way you can help him to not make the same mistake again.

WANT TO FULLY PREPARE FOR THE TRAIN DRIVER SELECTION?

This 1-day intensive training course is ideal for anyone who wants to ensure that they are fully prepared to pass the Trainee Train Driver selection process.

Understanding the role of a Train Driver and demonstrating the 'assessable' qualities.

Completing the application form correctly in order to ensure success.

Preparing for the psychometric tests.

Preparing for both sets of interview including a mock interview.

Rail recruitment information and where/how to apply.

FOR MORE INFORMATION ON OUR TRAIN DRIVER COURSE, PLEASE VISIT

www.TrainDriverCourse.co.uk

  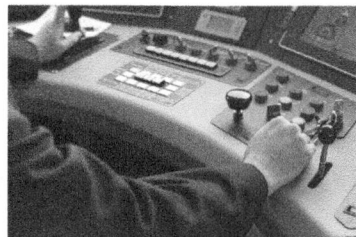

Get Access To
FREE
Psychometric Tests

www.PsychometricTestsOnline.co.uk

Printed and bound by CPI Group (UK) Ltd, Croydon, CR0 4YY
20/03/2026
02075172-0018